Ready for Adolescence Family Nights Tool Chest

Creating Lasting Impressions for the Next Generation!

Jim and Janet Weidmann

with Kurt Bruner

Cook Communications

Heritage Builders

I lovingly dedicate this book to the most important people in my life:
First of all, to my sweet husband, Jim, who has been so intentional to pass on a spiritual heritage to our children. Thank you for being my soul mate, my parenting partner, and a best friend. Also I dedicate this to my godly children: Josh, Jake, Janae, and Joy. You have blessed my life more than you will ever know. I am so thankful to know that we will spend eternity together. And finally, I dedicate this book to my parents, Bill and Marian Donaldson, who gave me my spiritual foundation and were responsible for my relationship with my Heavenly Father. Thank you all for blessing my life. I love you.

—Janet Weidmann

I want to give special acknowledgment to Dr. James Dobson for this book. I, as millions of others, have reaped the many blessings from his parenting insights. One of the "traditions" in our home is to take our children away for a "Preparing for Adolescence" weekend using Dr. Dobson's tape series. The principles presented made as big an impact on Janet and my life as they did on each of our children. Therefore, I wanted to draw from these life-changing points to help parents better equip their children through the Family Night Tool Chest series. I highly recommend that the next step with your adolescent after this book is to acquire the *Preparing for Adolescence* materials (p. 128). Then schedule the time—a weekend or a series of evenings—and work through the PFA resources to further develop these principles. Adolescence is a very impressionable time in a child's life. You need to be the one driving your child's understanding and perspectives, rather than the culture with it's many negative influences.
These tools by Dr. Dobson equip you to do just that!!

—Jim Wiedmann

Faith Parenting is an imprint of
Cook Communications Ministries, Colorado Springs, Colorado 80918
Cook Communications, Paris, Ontario
Kingsway Communications, Eastbourne, England

HERITAGE BUILDERS™/FAMILY NIGHTS TOOL CHEST—READY FOR ADOLESCENCE ™
© 2001 by Jim and Janet Weidmann, and Kurt Bruner

First Printing, 2001
Printed in the United States of America

1 2 3 4 5 6 7 8 9 10 Printing/Year 05 04 03 02 01

Editors: Steve Parolini and Craig Bubeck
Cover Design and Interior Illustrations: Guy Wolek
Design: Bill Gray
Interior Layout: Pat Miller

ISBN 0-78143-442-4

Heritage Builders/Family Nights Tool Chest—Ready for Adolescence is a Heritage Builders™ book.
To learn more about Heritage Builders, log on to our website at www.heritagebuilders.com.

Contents

Family Nights about Being Ready for Adolescence

The Heritage Builders™ Series

Family Nights Tool Chest was designed to motivate and assist families as they become intentional about the heritage passing process. This series draws upon the collective wisdom of parents, grandparents, church leaders, and family life experts, in an effort to provide balanced, biblical parenting advice along with effective, practical tools for family living.

Kurt Bruner, M.A.
Executive Editor
Heritage Builders™ Series

Introduction

There is toothpaste all over the plastic-covered table. Four young kids are having the time of their lives squeezing the paste out of the tube—trying to expunge every drop like Dad told them to. "Okay," says Dad, slapping a twenty-dollar bill onto the table. "The first person to get the toothpaste back into their tube gets this money!" Little hands begin working to shove the peppermint pile back into rolled-up tubes—with very limited success.

Jim is in the midst of a weekly routine in the Weidmann home when he and his wife spend time creating "impression points" with the kids. "We can't do it, Dad!" protests the youngest child.

"The Bible tells us that's just like your tongue. Once the words come out, it's impossible to get them back in. You need to be careful what you say because you may wish you could take it back." An unforgettable impression is made.

Impression points occur every day of our lives. Intentionally or not, we impress upon our children our values, preferences, beliefs, quirks, and concerns. It happens both through our talk and through our walk. When we do it right, we can turn them on to the things we believe. But when we do it wrong, we can turn them off to the values we most hope they will embrace. The goal is to find ways of making this reality work for us, rather than against us. How? By creating and capturing opportunities to impress upon the next generation our values and beliefs. In other words, through what we've labeled impression points.

The kids are all standing at the foot of the stairs. Jim is at the top of that same staircase. They wait eagerly for Dad's instructions.

"I'll take you to Baskin Robbins for ice cream if you can figure how to get up here." He has the attention of all four kids. "But there are a few rules. First, you can't touch the stairs. Second, you can't touch the railing. Now, begin!"

After several contemplative moments, the youngest speaks up. "That's impossible, Dad! How can we get to where you are without

touching the stairs or the railing?"

After some disgruntled agreement from two of the other children, Jacob gets an idea. "Hey, Dad. Come down here." Jim walks down the stairs. "Now bend over while I get on your back. Okay, climb the stairs."

Bingo! Jim proceeds to parallel this simple game with how it is impossible to get to God on our own. But when we trust Christ's completed work on our behalf, we can get to heaven. A lasting impression is made. After a trip up the stairs on Dad's back, the whole gang piles into the minivan for a double scoop of mint-chip.

Several years ago, Jim and his wife Janet began setting aside time to intentionally impress upon the kids their values and beliefs through a weekly ritual called "family night." They play games, talk, study, and do the things which reinforce the importance of family and faith. It is during these times that they intentionally create these impression points with their kids. The impact? The kids are having fun and a heritage is being passed.

☙ intentional or "oops"?

Sometimes, we accidentally impress the wrong things on our kids rather than intentionally impressing the right things. But there is an effective, easy way to change that. Routine family nights are a powerful tool for creating intentional impression points with our children.

The concept behind family nights is rooted in a biblical mandate summarized in Deuteronomy 6:5-9.

> *"Love the LORD your God with all your heart and with all your soul and with all your strength. These commandments that I give you today are to be upon your hearts. Impress them on your children."*
> *How?*
> *"Talk about them when you sit at home and when you walk along the road, when you lie down and when you get up. Tie them as symbols on your hands and bind them on your foreheads. Write them on the doorframes of your houses and on your gates."*

In other words, we need to take advantage of every opportunity to impress our beliefs and values in the lives of our children. A growing network of parents are discovering family nights to be a highly effective, user-friendly approach to doing just that. As one father put it, "This has changed our entire family life." And another dad, "Our investment of time and energy into family nights has more eternal value than we may ever know." Why? Because they are intentionally teaching their children at the wisdom level, the level at which the children understand and can apply eternal truths.

⊚ truth is a treasure

Two boys are running all over the house, carefully following the complex and challenging instructions spelled out on the "truth treasure map" they received moments ago. An earlier map contained a few rather simple instructions that were much easier to follow. But the "false treasure box" it lead to left something to be desired. It was empty. Boo Dad! They hope for a better result with map number two.

STEP ONE:

Walk sixteen paces into the front family room.

STEP TWO:

Spin around seven times, then walk down the stairs.

STEP THREE:

Run backwards to the other side of the room.

STEP FOUR:

Try and get around Dad and climb under the table.

You get the picture. The boys are laughing at themselves, complaining to Dad, and having a ball. After twenty minutes of treasure hunting they finally reach the elusive "truth treasure box." Little hands open the lid, hoping for a better result this time around. They aren't disappointed. The box contains a nice selection of their favorite candies. Yea Dad!

"Which map was easier to follow?" Dad asks.

"The first one," comes their response.

"Which one was better?"

"The second one. It led to a true treasure," says the oldest.

"That's just like life," Dad shares. "Sometimes it's easier to follow what is false. But it is always better to seek and follow what is true."

They read from Proverbs 2 about the hidden treasure of God's truth and end their time repeating tonight's jingle—"It's best for you to seek what's true." Then they indulge themselves with a mouthful of delicious candy!

☙ the power of family nights

The power of family nights is twofold. First, it creates a formal setting within which Dad and Mom can intentionally instill beliefs, values, or character qualities within their child. Rather than defer to the influence of peers and media, or abdicate character training to the school and church, parents create the opportunity to teach their children the things that matter most.

The second impact of family nights is perhaps even more significant than the first. Twenty to sixty minutes of formal fun and instruction can set up countless opportunities for informal reinforcement. These informal impression points do not have to be created, they just happen—at the dinner table, while driving in the car, while watching television, or any other parent/child time together. Once you have formally discussed a given family night topic, you and your children will naturally refer back to those principles during the routine dialogues of everyday life.

If the truth were known, many of us hated family devotions while growing up. We had them sporadically at best, usually whenever our parents were feeling particularly guilty. But that was fine, since the only thing worse was a trip to the dentist. Honestly, do we really think that is what God had in mind when He instructed us to teach our children? As an alternative, many parents are discovering family nights to be a wonderful complement to or replacement for family devotions as a means of passing their beliefs and values to the kids. In fact, many parents hear their kids ask at least three times per week:

"Can we have family night tonight?"

Music to Dad's and Mom's ears!

⊙ Keys to Effective Family Nights

There are several keys which should be incorporated into effective family nights.

MAKE IT FUN!

Enjoy yourself, and let the kids have a ball. They may not remember everything you say, but they will always cherish the times of laughter—and so will you.

KEEP IT SIMPLE!

The minute you become sophisticated or complicated, you've missed the whole point. Don't try to create deeply profound lessons. Just try to reinforce your values and beliefs in a simple, easy-to-understand manner. Read short passages, not long, drawn-out sections of Scripture. Remember: The goal is to keep it simple.

DON'T DOMINATE!

You want to pull them into the discovery process as much as possible. If you do all the talking, you've missed the mark. Ask questions, give assignments, invite participation in every way possible. They will learn more when you involve all of their senses and emotions.

GO WITH THE FLOW!

It's fine to start with a well-defined outline, but don't kill spontaneity by becoming overly structured. If an incident or question leads you in a different direction, great! Some of the best impression opportunities are completely unplanned and unexpected.

MIX IT UP!

Don't allow yourself to get into a rut or routine. Keep the sense of excitement and anticipation through variety. Experiment to discover what works best for your family. Use books, games, videos, props, made-up stories, songs, music or music videos, or even go on a family outing.

DO IT OFTEN!

We tend to find time for the things that are really important. It is best to set aside one evening per week (the same evening if possible) for family night. Remember, repetition is the best teacher. The more impressions you can create, the more of an impact you will make.

MAKE A MEMORY!

Find ways to make the lesson stick. For example, just as advertisers create "jingles" to help us remember their products, it is helpful to create family night "jingles" to remember the main theme—such as "It's best for you to seek what's true" or "Just like air, God is there!"

USE OTHER TOOLS FROM THE HERITAGE BUILDERS TOOL CHEST!

Family night is only one exciting way for you to intentionally build a loving heritage for your family. You'll also want to use these other exciting tools from Heritage Builders.

The Family Fragrance: There are five key qualities to a healthy family fragrance, each contributing to an environment of love in the home. It's easy to remember the Fragrance Five by fitting them into an acrostic using the word "Aroma"—

A—Affection
R—Respect
O—Order
M—Merriment
A—Affirmation

Family Moments: Ways that we impress on our children our values, preferences, and concerns. We do it through our talk and our actions. We do it intentionally (through such methods as Family Nights), and we do it incidentally.

Family Compass: Family Compass is the standard of normal healthy living against which our children will be able to measure their attitudes, actions, and beliefs.

Family Traditions: Meaningful activities which promote the process of passing on emotional, spiritual, and relational inheritance between generations. Family traditions can play a vital role in this process.

◎ How to Use This Tool Chest

Summary page: For those who like the bottom line, we have provided a summary sheet at the start of each family night session. This abbreviated version of the topic briefly highlights the goal, key Scriptures, activity overview, main points, and life slogan. On the reverse side of this detachable page there is space provided for you to write down any ideas you wish to add or alter as you make the lesson your own.

Step-by-step: For those seeking suggestions and directions for each step in the family night process, we have provided a section which walks you through every activity, question, Scripture reading, and discussion point. Feel free to follow each step as written as you conduct the session, or read through this portion in preparation for your time together.

À la carte: We strongly encourage you to use the material in this book in an "à la carte" manner. In other words, pick and choose the questions, activities, Scriptures, age-appropriate ideas, etc. which best fit your family. This book is not intended to serve as a curriculum, requiring compliance with our sequence and plan, but rather as a tool chest from which you can grab what works for you and which can be altered to fit your family situation.

The long and the short of it: Each family night topic presented in this book includes several activities, related Scriptures, and possible discussion items. Do not feel it is necessary to conduct them all in a single family night. You may wish to spread one topic over several weeks using smaller portions of each chapter, depending upon the attention span of the kids and the energy level of the parents. Remember, short and effective is better than long and thorough.

Journaling: Finally, we have provided space with each session for you to capture a record of meaningful comments, funny happenings, and unplanned moments which will inevitably occur during family night. Keep a notebook of these journal entries for future reference. You will treasure this permanent record of the heritage passing process for years to come.

☺ 1: Adolescence 101

Presenting the importance of discussing the adolescence stage

Scripture
• Luke 2:52
• Proverbs 1:8-9

ACTIVITY OVERVIEW		
Activity	Summary	Pre-Session Prep
Activity 1: Straw Tower	Learn how life gets more challenging as you grow into adolescence.	You'll need soda straws (50 or so per child) and a Bible.
Activity 2: You Can't Go Back	Learn the importance of trusting parents' wise advice.	You'll need a few bricks, blindfolds, a couple 2X4s, and a Bible.

Main Points

—We must grow and develop as Jesus did—physically, mentally, spiritually, and socially.

—It's important to talk about issues you'll be facing in adolescence before they come up, so you'll be prepared to face them.

LIFE VERSE: "Listen, my son, to your father's instruction and do not forsake your mother's teaching. They will be a garland to grace your head and a chain to adorn your neck" (Prov. 1:8-9).

Make it your own
In the space provided below, outline the flow and add any additional ideas to guide you through the process of conducting this family night.

Prayer & Praise Items
In the space provided below, list any items you wish to pray about or give praise for during this family night session.

Journal
In the space provided below, capture a record of any fun or meaningful things which happened during this family night session.

Session Tip

We intentionally have provided more material than we would expect to be used in a single "Family Night" session. You know your family's unique interests and life circumstances best, so feel free to adapt this lesson to meet your family members' needs. Remember, short and simple is better than long and comprehensive.

WARM-UP

Open with Prayer: Begin by having a family member pray, asking God to help everyone in the family understand more about Him through this time. After prayer, review your last lesson by asking these questions:

- **What did we learn about in our last lesson?**
- **What was the life verse?**
- **Have your actions changed because of what we learned? If so, how?** Encourage family members to give specific examples of how they've applied learning from the past week.

Share: Today we are going to learn why it's important to talk about adolescent issues before you become a teenager.

ACTIVITY 1: Straw Tower

Point: We must grow and develop as Jesus did—physically, mentally, spiritually, and socially.

 Supplies: You'll need soda straws (50 or so per child) and a Bible

Activity: Give each child a large supply of soda straws (at least 50 per child). Explain that he or she is to use the straws to build the tallest free-standing tower possible. If you have more than one child, you may want to make this into a contest—if not, repeat the activity to see if the child can improve upon his or her first tower attempt.

 After allowing time for the tower-building, consider the following questions:
- **What was it like to try to build a tower out of straws?** (It wasn't easy; it got harder as the tower grew.)
- **What challenges did you face as the tower got taller?** (It kept falling down; I had to build a bigger base.)
- **What did you find interesting about this exercise?** (It was fun to build something; I liked the challenge.)
- **In what ways was building the tower frustrating?** (It kept falling down; it was tough.)

Share: As you were building your tower, you probably had mixed feelings of excitement and frustration. Those same feelings are pretty normal for children who are almost teenagers. For example, you'll probably feel pretty excited about driving a car for the first time—and pretty frustrated as you try to remember all of the little rules of the road!

 If appropriate, share a few personal stories, recounting your own excitement and frustration while growing toward adolescence. Then have a family member **read** Luke 2:52.

 Ask:
- **What does this verse tell us about Jesus?** (He had to grow up, just like any other human; he faced adolescence too.)
- **In what ways did Jesus grow?** (*In wisdom*—intelligence and the skill of applying it; *in stature*—physical size and strength; *in favor with men*—social skills; and *in favor with God*—spiritual intimacy with God.)
- **How is the way we grow like and unlike the way your tower grew?** (It's similar because we grow a little at a time; it's different because we can grow without falling down so much.)

Share: Even though He was God, Jesus had a childhood and faced some of the same feelings of excitement and frustration. Though He didn't have the joy of looking forward to driving, he did have lots of great things to look forward to. And all of them had both freedom and responsibility attached.

Have children share some of the freedoms they're looking forward to and the accompanying responsibilities. Here are a few examples:

Freedom	Responsibility
Driving	Be safe and avoid hurting self or others
Socializing	Honor God with actions
Dating	Remain sexually pure
Work	Honor God by submitting to authority
Education	Grow in knowledge and wisdom

 Ask:

- **What are your greatest fears as you grow into adolescence?** (Will I have any friends; How will I fit in; Will I ever have a girl-friend/boyfriend.)

Share: The physical growth you're experiencing is unavoidable. But to grow spiritually, mentally, and socially, you will need the help of God's Word, good friends, and wisdom from your parents. You're not alone in this time of great change!

Age Adjustments

YOUNG CHILDREN can participate in the tower activity to add to the challenge for the older child or children, but won't benefit much from the discussion that follows. When you begin your discussion time, consider having younger children play elsewhere—or spend the time trying to build towers or other objects with the straws.

ACTIVITY 2: You Can't Go Back

 Point: God has given us as parents the responsibility to be by your side and guide you through adolescence. Therefore, it is important that we spend time talking through the issues now and when they arise.

Supplies: You'll need four bricks, blindfolds, a couple of 2X4s, and a Bible.

Activity: Before beginning this activity, you'll need to prepare the room. Using bricks and 2X4s, prepare a simple two-part, balance beam obstacle course. Place one 2X4 across the bricks (stacked two-high) for the first part of the course. At one end of that balance beam, build a little platform (three bricks wide, two bricks high), and from there begin the second part of the course by laying a 2X4 on the floor, angled away from the balance beam, but accessible with about a six-inch gap for someone to step down.

When the course is ready (and before your children see it), blindfold one person and lead him or her to the balance beam across the bricks. Help him or her onto the beam, and then walk alongside for support as the participant attempts to cross the beam. Once the brick platform is reached, remove the upper 2X4. Then ask him or her to carefully step out and find the second 2X4 to walk across. This may be difficult (or nearly impossible) since the child won't know where to step. If your child slips onto the floor, stop the activity and remove the blindfold. If he or she makes it to the end, remove the blindfold at that time. If you have more than one child, repeat the activity for each. Make sure you stay near each person who walks the beam for safety and assistance.

 When each has attempted the course, form a circle and discuss the following questions.
- **Tell me what you felt as you tried this activity.** (I was nervous; it wasn't easy; I thought I would fall.)
- **Did it help that you knew I was nearby? Explain.** (Yes, I knew I could keep my balance; a little, but I worried that you might not be able to catch me.)
- **What did you think when you noticed I took away the first balance beam?** (I wondered why you did that; it surprised me; it made me realize I couldn't go back.)

Share: This activity is like entering adolescence. Walking the balance beam is a bit scary—and sometimes you don't know if you're going to stay on it. But just as I stood by you then, I'll stand by you as you go through the tough times of growing up.

- **If this activity is like growing up, what do you think the removed balance beam represents?** (That you can't go back in life; that you can't always tell where you've been.)

Share: The author of Proverbs, King Solomon, was considered one of the wisest men who ever lived. Let's see what he has to say about children growing up.

 Read Proverbs 1:8-9.
- **What do you think Solomon is telling us in these verses?** (To trust parents; that parents' advice is important.)
- **How is the message of this verse like what we demonstrated in the activity?** (You were beside me in the activity, and

you'll be with me as I grow; you gave me advice while I walked on the beam and will give advice as I grow up.)

Share: Solomon knew that it is difficult for children to grow up and make good choices. That's why he said it would be important to listen to parents. When you listen to parents' wisdom, you can be better prepared to face difficult situations in life (and not fall off life's balance beam).

Hug each child and make a commitment to be there for him or her and to offer your wisdom as needed.

WRAP-UP

Gather everyone in a circle and have family members take turns answering this question: **What's one thing you've learned about God today?**

Next, tell kids you have a "Life Verse" you'd like to share with them.

Age Adjustments

YOUNG CHILDREN will love trying the balance beam activity. Go ahead and allow them a turn, and if you have time, use this activity to discuss how having you nearby is like having God near as we go forward in life. This can be a great activity for very young children, too, as they can feel like they've done something really special.

Life Verse: Today's Life Verse is Proverbs 1:8-9. "Listen, my son, to your father's instruction and do not forsake your mother's teaching. They will be a garland to grace your head and a chain to adorn your neck." Have family members repeat the verses two or three times to help them learn it. Then encourage them to practice saying them during the week so they can talk about it at your next family night session.

Close in Prayer: Allow time for each family member to share prayer concerns and answers to prayer. Then close your time together with prayer for each concern. Thank God for listening to and caring about us.

Remember to record your prayer requests so you can refer to them in the future as you see God answering them.

☮ 2: Inferiority

Teaching children that it's normal to have feelings of inferiority as they grow through adolescence.

Scripture
- 1 Samuel 16:7
- Exodus 4:10-14; 20:16
- Psalm 139:13-16
- 1 Corinthians 12:7-11
- Jeremiah 29:11

ACTIVITY OVERVIEW		
Activity	Summary	Pre-Session Prep
Activity 1: Optical Illusions	Learn that God sees people differently than the world sees them.	You'll need copies of the "Optical Illusions" page and a Bible.
Activity 2: Inevitable Feelings	Learn that they're uniquely gifted and a product of God's creative hand.	You'll need balloons (not helium quality—the cheap ones work best), and a Bible.

Main Points

—God doesn't see us the way the world does—He looks at the heart.

—You are a product of God's hand, made in His image, and you are uniquely gifted.

LIFE VERSE: "For you created my inmost being; you knit me together in my mother's womb. I praise you because I am fearfully and wonderfully made; your works are wonderful, I know that full well. My frame was not hidden from you when I was made in the secret place. When I was woven together in the depths of the earth, your eyes saw my unformed body. All the days ordained for me were written in your book before one of them came to be" (Psalm 139:13-16).

Make it your own

In the space provided below, outline the flow and add any additional ideas to guide you through the process of conducting this family night.

Prayer & Praise Items

In the space provided below, list any items you wish to pray about or give praise for during this family night session.

Journal

In the space provided below, capture a record of any fun or meaningful things which happened during this family night session.

Session Tip

We intentionally have provided more material than we would expect to be used in a single "Family Night" session. You know your family's unique interests and life circumstances best, so feel free to adapt this lesson to meet your family members' needs. Remember, short and simple is better than long and comprehensive.

WARM-UP

Open with Prayer: Begin by having a family member pray, asking God to help everyone in the family understand more about Him through this time. After prayer, review your last lesson by asking these questions:

- **What did we learn in our last lesson?**
- **What was the life verse?**
- **Have your actions changed because of what we learned? If so, how?** Encourage family members to give specific examples of how they've applied learning from the past week.

Share: Today we are going to learn that it's normal to feel inferior—and that God sees us as excellent creatures.

ACTIVITY 1: Optical Illusions

Point: God doesn't see us the way the world does— He looks at the heart.

Supplies: You'll need copies of the "Optical Illusions" page (p. 24) and a Bible.

Activity: Photocopy the "Optical Illusions" page (p. 24) and give a copy to each family member. (Or you may simply pass the book around and let family members look at it one at a time.) Then consider the following questions.

- **What do you see on this page?** (Things that aren't what they seem; optical illusions.)
- **What makes these illusions?** (The wavy lines; the stuff around the objects.)
- **What seems right in one setting (school, sports, clubs, friends) may not be right according to God's values, which He's given us in the Bible.** (For example, friends normally will talk among themselves about others. But when they

Optical Illusions

A. Are the horizontal lines parallel?

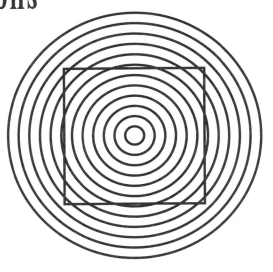

B. Are the square's edges straight?

C. Is there a spiral?

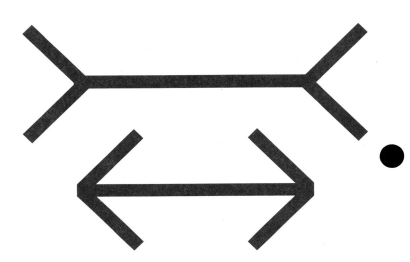

D. Which line is longer?

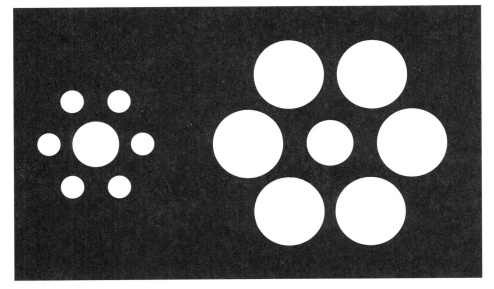

E. Which of the inner circles is bigger?

24

start to spread rumors about someone, Christians need to remember the ninth commandment—Ex. 20:16.)

● **Share: Just as the images were distorted by the surrounding lines, sometimes our view of things is distorted. For example, the world looks at the outward appearance and actions of a person. Let's try a little exercise to see how this works.**

 Have your children rapidly list the answers to the following questions before continuing:
- **Who is the best athlete in your class?**
- **Who is the most beautiful girl/guy?**
- **Who is the richest person in your class?**
- **Who is the smartest or most likely to succeed?**

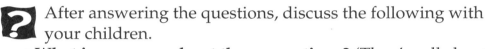 After answering the questions, discuss the following with your children.
- **What is common about these questions?** (They're all about outward appearance; none of them focuses on the person's character.)
- **Why do people look at outward things?** (Because it's easy; because TV and movies tell is it's important.)

●   **Read** aloud 1 Samuel 16:7; then discuss the following questions.
- **What does this passage tell us about how God sees people?** (He looks at the inside—a man's thoughts and intentions. He does not consider outward appearance.)
- **What can you learn from this verse that can help you deal with your peers?** (Don't choose friends based upon outward appearances; get to know a person before deciding anything about him or her.)

Share: Though the world's distortion of how we see people is hard to change, with God's help, we can begin to see people as He does—we can see people for who they are and not what they look like.

Age Adjustments

YOUNG CHILDREN **may have a hard time understanding the message of this activity, but certainly will enjoy the optical illusions. Give younger children paper and pencils and encourage them to create their own illusions while you work with your older children on the activity application.**

ACTIVITY 2: Inevitable Feelings

Point: You are a product of God's hand, made in His image, and you are uniquely gifted.

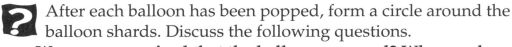

 Supplies: You'll need balloons (not helium quality—the cheap ones work best), and a Bible

Activity: Give each family member a balloon. Have family members blow up the balloons as much as possible without having them pop. Hold the balloons while blown up and compare sizes. Then have each person continue to blow up the balloons even more. Repeat this until the balloons pop. If someone in your family can't blow up the balloons or doesn't want to pop them, help them out by blowing them up and popping them yourself. (Note: eye protection should always be worn with such an activity.)

After each balloon has been popped, form a circle around the balloon shards. Discuss the following questions.

- **Were you surprised that the balloons popped? Why or why not?** (Yes, I didn't know you'd blow them up so much; no, that's what balloons do when they're under pressure.)
- **It was inevitable that the balloon would pop. What experiences are inevitable as you grow into a teenager?** (Physical changes; mood swings; not fitting in.)

Share: Just as a balloon eventually pops with too much air, certain feelings are inevitable for children as they enter adolescence. One of those feelings is inferiority—or feeling like you don't fit in.

Ask your child to share some of the things that might make him or her feel inferior. Here are a few possible answers:

- Not knowing what to say to a member of the opposite sex.
- Not being as strong or physically developed as other kids.
- Being too tall; too short; having acne or a changing voice.
- Not being sure how to relate to other students.

Share: You're not the only person who will have experienced feelings of inferiority. In fact, one famous Bible character felt pretty inferior—and then went on to do great things for God.

 Read Exodus 4:10-14. Then discuss the following question.
- **Why did Moses feel inferior?** (He couldn't speak well; he didn't have confidence.)

Share: Moses didn't think he was good enough to do what God asked of him. As you grow into adolescence, you'll probably feel like you're not good enough to accomplish things too.

Read Psalm 139:13-16, 1 Corinthians 12:7-11, and Jeremiah 29:11; then ask family members to tell how these verses can help people when they're feeling inferior.

Here are a few possible answers:
- God made us just as we are.
- God doesn't make mistakes.
- God gives each person special gifts.
- God has a plan for my life.

Share: You are a product of God's hand and made in His image. He has given you unique gifts and talents and has a great plan for your life. Whenever you're feeling like you don't fit in or like you're inferior to others, remember that God created you to be you—He sees you as a perfect creation!

Age Adjustments

YOUNG CHILDREN can learn a lesson of "being special" by using the balloons in a different way. Blow up a few extra balloons and tie them. Give children markers and have them draw self-portraits on the balloons. When done, spend a few minutes talking with small children about how each balloon is different and special and how that's true of them as well. Explain that God created each person to be "one of a kind" and that God loves His creation.

WRAP-UP

Gather everyone in a circle and have family members take turns answering this question: **What's one thing you've learned about God today?**

Next, tell kids you have a new "Life Verse" you'd like to share with them.

Life Verse: Today's Life Verse is Psalm 139:13-16. "For you created my inmost being; you knit me together in my mother's womb. I praise you because I am fearfully and

wonderfully made; your works are wonderful, I know that full well. My frame was not hidden from you when I was made in the secret place. When I was woven together in the depths of the earth, your eyes saw my unformed body. All the days ordained for me were written in your book before one of them came to be." Have family members repeat the verses two or three times to help them learn it. Then encourage them to practice saying them during the week so they can talk about it at your next family night session.

Close in Prayer: Allow time for each family member to share prayer concerns and answers to prayer. Then close your time together with prayer for each concern. Thank God for listening to and caring about us.

Remember to record your prayer requests so you can refer to them in the future as you see God answering them.

☺ 3: Never Alone

Teaching children that they're not alone as they face adolescence

Scripture
- Hebrews 13:5
- James 1:2-4

ACTIVITY OVERVIEW		
Activity	Summary	Pre-Session Prep
Activity 1: Shoe Snap	Learn that growing up is a "team" event.	You'll need strips of elastic, chairs, shoes, and a Bible.
Activity 2: Life Lessons	Discover that we can learn from difficult experiences.	You'll need a snap-together model or simple puzzle and a Bible.

Main Points

—You are not the only one with adolescent struggles.

—Problems are inevitable, but with God's help, we can learn from difficult experiences.

LIFE VERSE: "Keep your lives free from the love of money and be content with what you have, because God has said, 'Never will I leave you; never will I forsake you'" Hebrews 13:5.

Make it your own
In the space provided below, outline the flow and add any additional ideas to guide you through the process of conducting this family night.

Prayer & Praise Items
In the space provided below, list any items you wish to pray about or give praise for during this family night session.

Journal
In the space provided below, capture a record of any fun or meaningful things which happened during this family night session.

Session Tip

We intentionally have provided more material than we would expect to be used in a single "Family Night" session. You know your family's unique interests and life circumstances best, so feel free to adapt this lesson to meet your family members' needs. Remember, short and simple is better than long and comprehensive.

WARM-UP

Open with Prayer: Begin by having a family member pray, asking God to help everyone in the family understand more about Him through this time. After prayer, review your last lesson by asking these questions:

- **What did we learn about in our last lesson?**
- **What was the life verse?**
- **Have your actions changed because of what we learned? If so, how?** Encourage family members to give specific examples of how they've applied learning from the past week.

Share: Today we are going to learn that you're not alone as you face adolescence and that God is always with you.

ACTIVITY 1: Shoe Snap

Point: You are not alone in facing adolescent struggles.

 Supplies: You'll need strips of elastic (bungee cords), chairs, shoes, and a Bible

Activity: For this activity, you'll need to set two chairs about five feet apart, facing each other. Tie a piece of elastic onto each front leg of both chairs. Then tie the other ends of the elastic strips to big shoes (one pair for each chair). You'll need to have someone sitting in each chair so it won't slide. The object of the activity will be for children (or a parent and a child) to step into a pair of shoes, walk to the middle between the chairs, exchange shoes without allowing them to snap back, then walk over and sit down on the opposite chair. For this to be a fun game, the elastic must be stretched to its limit as participants are attempting to trade shoes.

Test the game first to determine the proper distance between chairs.

When your activity area is prepared, invite children into the room and explain the activity. Then have children try it. If you have two or more children, have them take turns playing. If you have one child, have a parent play along with the child.

If a shoe snaps back while playing the game, have players return to their starting chairs and try again.

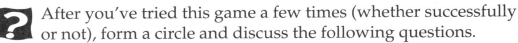 After you've tried this game a few times (whether successfully or not), form a circle and discuss the following questions.

- **How easy or difficult was this activity?** (It was tough, I kept losing the shoes; it was pretty easy because we worked well together.)
- **Was this a team or individual activity? Explain.** (A team activity—we had to work together.)
- **How did the experience of both players compare?** (It was basically the same for both; we each had the same challenge.)

If you have them, show your children pictures of you and your spouse around the ages of 12–14. After the giggles and laugher, talk together about some of the differences between you as a young adolescent and your child.

Age Adjustments

YOUNG CHILDREN can play along with this activity and enjoy the challenge of trading shoes with their older brother or sister. To turn this into a learning event for younger children, simply focus on the fact that they had to work together with a partner to accomplish the task. Explain how that's like working with a friend to do something of value. You could also make the application that God is our helper and can assist us in getting things done when we ask for His help.

Share: While things have certainly changed in the years since I was a young teenager, some things haven't changed. In fact, many of the same things you'll be facing your parents already faced! Just as we had the same challenges in this shoe snap game, teenagers today have similar challenges as those who were teenagers years ago. And just as we had to work together to accomplish the game, we'll have to work together to help you through the teenage years.

  Read Hebrews 13:5 and discuss the following questions.

- **What does this passage tell us about God's role as we go through adolescence?** (He'll always be there; He's our comforter.)

• **How can the message of this verse help you as you experience the ups and downs of becoming a teenager?** (I can feel comforted that God is near; I can know that God will be there even when I'm scared or embarrassed.)

Share: Even though other kids your age may not be sharing their feelings, they probably are experiencing many of the same things you are. Remember that you're not the only one going through these crazy times—and remember that you're not alone—God is with you!

ACTIVITY 2: Life Lessons

Point: Problems are inevitable, but with God's help, we can learn from difficult experiences.

 Supplies: You'll need a snap-together model or simple puzzle and a Bible

Activity: Give your children a simple snap-together model or a puzzle with less than 50 pieces and have them quickly put it together. Time each child and write down the total time it takes to complete the task. Then have them repeat the activity, keeping track of the time it takes to finish.

 When each child has completed the task at least twice, form a circle around the model or puzzle and consider the following questions.

• **How easy was it to complete the model (or puzzle)?** (It was pretty easy; I didn't get it right the first time.)
• **How did the ease of completion change with the second (or more) attempt?** (It got easier; I still messed up.)

 Read aloud James 1:2-4. Then ask:
• **What does this Bible passage tell us about trouble?** (It will come; we can learn from problems.)
• **How is the way you learned from the first model attempt like the way you learn from problems?** (I learned the consequences of my choices, so I could make better choices the next time.)

Share: Just as you learned from your mistakes and did a better job of putting the model together the second time,

we can learn from our mistakes (and other people's mistakes) in life and become stronger. That strength is often called character.

Have children list problems they think they might face in middle school and high school that could be tough challenges. Here are a few examples:
- Rejection by friends
- Being teased or called names
- Failing in a class or sports activity
- Breaking up with a boyfriend/girlfriend

Age Adjustments

YOUNG CHILDREN can get a simple lesson on the importance of learning from our mistakes by participating in this activity (or something similar). Choose a puzzle that is age-appropriate for younger children, and help them learn how to speed up the completion of the puzzle by seeing what they did wrong on the first attempt. After pointing out that they did a better job the second time, help them to see that the same principle is evident in our everyday lives (picking up a room, getting answers right at school, responding properly to friends or parents).

Have children share how each of these situations might help them build strong character. Then **share: Problems are inevitable in our lives. But with God's guidance, we can avoid many mistakes, and learn from those we do make as we develop our relationship with God and others.**

WRAP-UP

Gather everyone in a circle and have family members take turns answering this question: **What's one thing you've learned about God today?**

Next, tell kids you've got a new "Life Verse" you'd like to share with them.

Life Verse: Today's Life Verse is Hebrews 13:5. "Keep your lives free from the love of money and be content with what you have, because God has said, 'Never will I leave you; never will I forsake you.'" Have family members repeat the verse two or three times to help them learn it. Then encourage them to practice saying it during the week so they can talk about it at your next family night session.

Close in Prayer: Allow time for each family member to share prayer concerns and answers to prayer. Then close your time together with prayer for each concern. Thank God for listening to and caring about us.

Remember to record your prayer requests so you can refer to them in the future as you see God answering them.

@ 4: Why Wait?

Teaching children the importance of saving sex for marriage

Scripture
- 1 Corinthians 6:18-20
- 1 Thessalonians 4:3-8

ACTIVITY OVERVIEW		
Activity	Summary	Pre-Session Prep
Activity 1: Big Mess	Learn how some things that look good can have negative consequences.	You'll need cake donuts, string, a bowl, chocolate syrup, towels, and a Bible.
Activity 2: Commitment	Learn the importance of making a commitment.	You'll need paper, a pen or pencil, snacks, and a Bible.

Main Points

—God has given us sex as a gift only to be shared with our spouse.

—With the help of the Holy Spirit, we can choose to remain sexually pure.

LIFE VERSE: "Instead, you yourselves cheat and do wrong, and you do this to your brothers. Do you not know that the wicked will not inherit the kingdom of God? Do not be deceived: Neither the sexually immoral nor idolaters nor adulterers nor male prostitutes nor homosexual offenders nor thieves nor the greedy nor drunkards nor slanderers nor swindlers will inherit the kingdom of God" 1 Corinthians 6:8-10.

Make it your own
In the space provided below, outline the flow and add any additional ideas to guide you through the process of conducting this family night.

Prayer & Praise Items
In the space provided below, list any items you wish to pray about or give praise for during this family night session.

Journal
In the space provided below, capture a record of any fun or meaningful things which happened during this family night session.

Session Tip

We intentionally have provided more material than we would expect to be used in a single "Family Night" session. You know your family's unique interests and life circumstances best, so feel free to adapt this lesson to meet your family members' needs. Remember, short and simple is better than long and comprehensive.

WARM-UP

Open with Prayer: Begin by having a family member pray, asking God to help everyone in the family understand more about Him through this time. After prayer, review your last lesson by asking these questions:

- **What did we learn about in our last lesson?**
- **What was the life verse?**
- **Have your actions changed because of what we learned? If so, how?** Encourage family members to give specific examples of how they've applied learning from the past week.

Share: Today we are going to learn why it's important to save sex for marriage.

ACTIVITY 1: Big Mess

Point: God has given us sex as a gift only to be shared with our spouse.

 Supplies: You'll need cake donuts, string, a bowl, chocolate syrup, towels, and a Bible.

Activity: Lay a towel on the floor where you'll be doing this activity. Since this could be a rather messy activity, choose a room where cleanup will be easy. Next to the towel, place a bowl of chocolate syrup. Then carefully tie a small doughnut to a long string and invite a family member to lie down, with his or her head on the towel. Explain that the object of the game is to eat the donut while you dangle it over your child's face. Tell children that they're to see if they can eat the whole thing without allowing any of it to drop to the floor.

Just before you dangle the donut above your child's face, dip it into the chocolate sauce. Then, using the string, hold it about an inch or two above your child's mouth. This can be a fun activity to watch, so make sure all family members are in the room and enjoying the messy event.

After the first family member has attempted to eat a donut, repeat the activity for each other family member. For fun, take a picture of your children's chocolate-covered faces before cleaning up.

 After cleaning up, consider discussing the following questions with your adolescent child.

- **What were your thoughts about this activity?** (It sure was messy; the donut tasted good.)
- **Was it possible to eat the donut and not get messy? Why or why not?** (No, because the chocolate sauce kept dripping on my face; no, because the donut kept breaking.)
- **How might this activity be what it's like to have sex before marriage?** (Just like donuts were not meant to be eaten this way, sex was never intended to be outside of marriage. It might look good, but you can end up in a mess; there's no way to enjoy it fully as intended.)
- **What does the world say about sex before marriage?** (It's okay if you really love the person; it's dangerous because of disease; you should take birth control.)

Share: Sex is an intimate experience—one that's not easily forgotten. And it's a gift that God gave to couples who are committed to each other in marriage. Have you ever discovered a present that you were getting before Christmas morning? It probably felt pretty exciting to see what you'd be getting . . . but on Christmas morning, the excitement was gone. The same is true for sex. Sex is a gift designed for two people to discover together on their wedding night.

  Read 1 Corinthians 6:18-20. Then discuss the following questions.

- **What does this passage tell us about sex outside of marriage?** (It's a sin; it can negatively affect your body; we must honor God with our bodies.)
- **How does this passage compare to the world's view of sex?** (The world says sex is okay as long as it's safe; the world doesn't see sex outside of marriage as a sin.)

Share: God had a good idea when He created sex . . . but people have messed up that idea. God's gift of sex is like a delicious donut—but unless people wait until their wedding night to enjoy it, they're going to face all kinds of messy problems (such as guilt, disease, and pregnancy).

ACTIVITY 2: Commitment

Point: With the help of the Holy Spirit, we can choose to remain sexually pure.

 Supplies: You'll need a pen, string, a paper clip, and a bottle.

Activity: Tie one end of a 1- to 2-foot string (depending on the size of the child—you want the pen to hang just above the knees) to a paper clip, and the other end to the pen. With the paper clip, attach the string to the back of the child's pants. Place an empty bottle in the middle of the floor. The object of the game is to get the pen in the bottle. The problem is that when trying to aim from an upside down perspective, while sighting between one's legs, it is more difficult than it might seem to position the pen directly over the bottle's opening.

- **Was the game hard?** (Yes; I could not see from the right angle/perspective to line up the pen with the bottle.)
- **How do you think this is like the world's perspective of commitment versus God's view of commitment when it comes to sex?** (The world tells you that it is okay to have sex without the marriage commitment—that simply feeling love for another is reason enough. God tells you that sex is designed for marriage alone, which is a relationship that should last until the death of a spouse.)

Emphasize that the marriage vow is not only a commitment before the spouse and all people present, but before God. Sex was given for marriage, so your commitment to marriage starts now—not at the altar. Waiting to have sex before marriage is called purity or chastity, and keeping sex within your marriage is called integrity. Clearly your commitment to purity before the day of marriage is important to God, just as is integrity after marriage.

Age Adjustments

YOUNG CHILDREN should not participate in the discussions following the donut activity. You'll want to plan a separate activity for them during your talk with your older children. If you'd like to make an application from the activity that the younger children can take with them, consider comparing the mess made while trying to get the donut to the mess we get into when we do something that seems like fun—but is wrong (such as taking a toy from another or disobeying). You might want to consider having the younger children meet with one parent for the debriefing while another talks with the adolescent.

 **Read** 1 Thessalonians 4:3-8 and discuss the following questions.

- **What does this passage challenge us to do regarding sex?** (Stay away from sexual sin; be pure; honor God.)
- **How can we do what this passage advises?** (Make a commitment to stay pure; ask for God's help to avoid sexual sin.)

Share: God wants you to make a commitment to be sexually pure so the gift of sex can be enjoyed in a marriage relationship. Let's write a commitment that will help you see what kinds of things are important to control in order to stay pure.

Work together to write up a commitment. Consider the following topics as you work on this with your children.

- **Commitment to control our thoughts** (avoid movies, TV shows with sexual content; stay away from pornography; abstain from telling dirty jokes; pray for God's help when tempted)
- **Commitment to control our situations** (avoid drinking alcohol, stay away from unsupervised parties, leave when tempted by situations or surroundings; determine limits to physical contact while dating, and stick to them)
- **Commitment to being accountable** (choose a Christian friend who will keep you accountable; talk with parents openly and honestly about fears, temptations, and challenges)
- **Commitment to dating others who know Christ** (avoid getting serious with non-Christians because of "unequal yoke"; seek romantic relationships only with those who live by God's rules)

When you've created a commitment, read it together and then, if you can agree with its content, have older children and parents sign and date it. Keep this commitment in a safe place, and review it from time to time with your older children.

At the end of this activity, enjoy the snack you committed to earlier. Make a special point of how keeping a commitment is something to be celebrated and how God loves a kept commitment.

NOTE: Making a commitment is no easy task for adolescents, who know very little of what it means to be stable and secure. With raging hormones and daily challenges of peer pressure, they'll need your constant support, prayer, and wisdom to keep this commitment. Should your child err and break the commitment, shower the child with love and remind him or her of God's forgiveness and the ability to wipe the slate clean. Then begin again, perhaps with a tighter accountability system if needed.

WRAP-UP

Gather everyone in a circle and have family members take turns answering this question: **What's one thing you've learned about God today?**

Next, tell kids you've got a new "Life Verse" you'd like to share with them.

Life Verse: Today's Life Verse is 1 Corinthians 6:8-10. "Instead, you yourselves cheat and do wrong, and you do this to your brothers. Do you not know that the wicked will not inherit the kingdom of God? Do not be deceived: Neither the sexually immoral nor idolaters nor adulterers nor male prostitutes nor homosexual offenders nor thieves nor the greedy nor drunkards nor slanderers nor swindlers will inherit the kingdom of God." Have family members repeat the verses two or three times to help them learn it. Then encourage them to practice saying them during the week so they can talk about it at your next family night session.

Close in Prayer: Allow time for each family member to share prayer concerns and answers to prayer. Then close your time together with prayer for each concern. Thank God for listening to and caring about us.

Remember to record your prayer requests so you can refer to them in the future as you see God answering them.

Age Adjustments

YOUNG CHILDREN again will need to have a separate discussion time during this activity. To simplify the message of this activity, change "commitment" to "promise" and help younger children see the importance of keeping our promises (to clean a room, help a friend, or complete a chore). You might even write up a simple "promise paper" together that is a commitment to following through with the things you say you'll do. This kind of early exposure to following through on promises can translate into a better understanding of commitment as younger children grow toward adolescence.

@ 5: More Than a Feeling

Teaching children that love is more than a feeling

Scripture
- 1 Corinthians 13:4-8
- 2 Samuel 13:1-2, 14-15
- Proverbs 3:5-6

ACTIVITY OVERVIEW		
Activity	Summary	Pre-Session Prep
Activity 1: What Do You See?	Learn the difference between infatuation and love.	You'll need soft drinks (such as colas and root-beer), coffee, tea, paper cups, and a Bible.
Activity 2: Which Way Will It Go?	Learn that mood swings are a part of adolescence.	You'll need balloons and a Bible.

Main Points

— Love is bigger than first impressions—it involves commitment, forgiveness, understanding, and sacrifice.

— Mood swings are a part of adolescence, but when we focus on God, everything regains proper balance.

LIFE VERSES: "Trust in the LORD with all your heart and lean not on your own understanding; in all your ways acknowledge him, and he will make your paths straight" Proverbs 3:5-6.

Make it your own

In the space provided below, outline the flow and add any additional ideas to guide you through the process of conducting this family night.

Prayer & Praise Items

In the space provided below, list any items you wish to pray about or give praise for during this family night session.

Journal

In the space provided below, capture a record of any fun or meaningful things which happened during this family night session.

Session Tip

We intentionally have provided more material than we would expect to be used in a single "Family Night" session. You know your family's unique interests and life circumstances best, so feel free to adapt this lesson to meet your family members' needs. Remember, short and simple is better than long and comprehensive.

 WARM-UP

Open with Prayer: Begin by having a family member pray, asking God to help everyone in the family understand more about Him through this time. After prayer, review your last lesson by asking these questions:

- **What did we learn in our last lesson?**
- **What was the life verse?**
- **Have your actions changed because of what we learned? If so, how?** Encourage family members to give specific examples of how they've applied learning from the past week.

Share: Today we are going to learn that it's normal to have mixed-up feelings as you move into adolescence. But with God's help, you can balance those highs and lows.

ACTIVITY 1: What do You See?

Point: Love is bigger than first impressions—it involves commitment, forgiveness, understanding, and sacrifice.

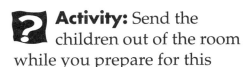 **Supplies:** You'll need soft drinks (such as colas and rootbeer), coffee, tea, paper cups, and a Bible

Activity: Send the children out of the room while you prepare for this activity. Fill four or more cups with different dark-colored drinks (such as rootbeer, various colas, and coffee). Set the cups on a table. Then, one at a time, invite family members into the room and have them guess what's in each cup (only by looking at them from a few feet away). You might want to write their guesses on a sheet of paper so they can learn how well they guessed. Repeat this activity with all family members; then have everyone enter the room. Consider the following question.

- **Can you tell what each of these drinks is by looking at it? Why or why not?** (No, they all look the same; I can tell some of them.)

Have children sample the drinks and determine what's in each cup. Compare this to family members' guesses. Then continue your discussion time by considering the following.

Share: Just as you couldn't know what was in these cups until you tasted them, you can't know someone well until you've really invested some time with them. As you approach adolescence you're probably going to have feelings of infatuation, which means being attracted to and thinking highly of someone without really knowing him or her. This is a normal feeling, but it's usually based on a person's outward appearance and can be lustful.

Have a volunteer read a definition of "lust" from a dictionary. Then **read** about Amnon in 2 Samuel 13:1-2, 14-15. Help your older children see that Amnon's "infatuation" turned to lust, and lust to hate. While this is an extreme example, it is valuable to show children how lust can be destructive in relationships.

Share: Amnon believed he loved someone, but he was probably just attracted to her because of her outward appearance. Infatuation is a pretty normal feeling for teenagers, but it become a problem when that infatuation becomes lustful or sexual desire.

 Read 1 Corinthians 13:4-8. Then ask.
- **What does this passage tell us about love?** (Love is patient and kind; love is not self-serving; love lasts forever.)
- **Based on this, and what we've learned about infatuation, what is the difference between love and infatuation?** (Love takes time; infatuation will pass; love looks out for the other person's interests and needs.)

Share: Infatuation and lust are easily confused with love. The big difference is that infatuation and lust are self-centered, while love is other-centered. Love involves commitment, forgiveness, understanding, and sacrifice. With God's guidance, we can build relationships upon true love and concern for the other person.

ACTIVITY 2: Which Way Will It Go?

Point: Mood swings are a part of adolescence; but focusing upon God gives proper balance.

 Supplies: balloons and a Bible.

Activity: You'll probably want to do this activity outdoors (or in a large basement). Mark a "starting" and "finish" line approximately 25 feet apart. Give each family member an uninflated balloon. Explain that the object of the game is to get the balloon over the finish line by blowing it up and releasing it. Wherever the balloon lands, they're to blow it up and release it again. Explain that they need to continue until they get the balloon across the finish line. (This could take a few turns, as the balloon will fly unpredictably.)

If you have one child, you may repeat the activity a few times, keeping track of the time (or turns) it takes to complete the task. Otherwise, make this a competition to see who can cross the line fastest (or with fewest turns). After the fun, discuss the following questions with your older children.

- **What made this game difficult to complete?** (The balloon didn't go straight; we didn't know where the balloon would land.)
- **How might this balloon be like emotions during adolescence?** (Our feelings change a lot; we have lots of highs and lows; feelings are unpredictable.)
- **What kinds of situations might you face that could cause rapidly changing emotions?** (Dating or getting dumped; doing poorly in sports or academics; finding or losing a good friend; being teased; getting a great grade on a test.)

Age Adjustments

YOUNG CHILDREN can play the "drink guessing" game, but take them aside for a different kind of debriefing. Consider using this activity to explore how appearances can be deceiving. For example, you could talk with your child about how we can't really know someone based on how he or she looks. This might be helpful for children who are uncomfortable around people who seem different from them.

 Read aloud Proverbs 3:5-6 and ask family members to tell you what this passage is all about. Allow time for discussion.

Share: Just as the balloon flew unpredictably around the room, as you grow you'll face emotional highs and lows that you can't predict. That's normal. But if we will trust God, we can find hope and strength to stay balanced even when life seems out of control. We should not focus on ourselves, our failures, our accomplishments, or even on a relationship that has gone bad. For our hope is only found in Him, not in other people, things, or events. God can make sense out of our unpredictable paths . . . and He can straighten them out too!

WRAP-UP

Gather everyone in a circle and have family members take turns answering: **What's one thing you've learned about God today?**

Next, tell kids you have new "Life Verses" you'd like to share with them.

Life Verses: Today's Life Verses are Proverbs 3:5-6 Trust in the LORD with all your heart and lean not on your own understanding; in all your ways acknowledge him, and he will make your paths straight." Have family members repeat the verses two or three times to help them learn them. Then encourage them to practice saying them during the week so they can talk about them at your next family night session.

Close in Prayer: Allow time for each family member to share prayer concerns and answers to prayer. Then close your time together with prayer for each concern. Thank God for listening to and caring about us.

Remember to record your prayer requests so you can refer to them in the future as you see God answering them.

Age Adjustments

YOUNG CHILDREN will love the balloon activity. Go ahead and play it a few times with them. But since younger children need a sense of stability, don't focus your discussion with them on the unpredictability of feelings or emotions. Instead, simply use this activity to help younger children learn that life is filled with surprises. This could be a good time to talk about how God sometimes surprises us with new friends, a new school, a new job, and so on. Through your discussion, children might become better prepared to expect the unexpected.

6:Friendships

Teaching children the importance of true friends

Scripture
- Proverbs 27:17
- James 2:14, 17
- 1 Samuel 18:1-4; 23:16-18
- 1 Corinthians 16:13

ACTIVITY OVERVIEW

Activity	Summary	Pre-Session Prep
Activity 1: Friend or Foe?	Learn the importance of choosing true friends.	You'll need a Bible.
Activity 2: Shaping Your Witness	Learn to be courageous in your faith.	You'll need pipe cleaners and a Bible.

Main Points

—Choose friends who will encourage your walk with God.

—Be courageous in your faith so you can be a strong witness for Christ.

LIFE VERSE: "Be on your guard; stand firm in the faith; be men of courage; be strong."
1 Corinthians 16:13.

Make it your own

In the space provided below, outline the flow and add any additional ideas to guide you through the process of conducting this family night.

Prayer & Praise Items

In the space provided below, list any items you wish to pray about or give praise for during this family night session.

Journal

In the space provided below, capture a record of any fun or meaningful things which happened during this family night session.

Session Tip

We intentionally have provided more material than we would expect to be used in a single "Family Night" session. You know your family's unique interests and life circumstances best, so feel free to adapt this lesson to meet your family members' needs. Remember, short and simple is better than long and comprehensive.

WARM-UP

Open with Prayer: Begin by having a family member pray, asking God to help everyone in the family understand more about Him through this time. After prayer, review your last lesson by asking these questions:

- **What did we learn about in our last lesson?**
- **What was the life verse?**
- **Have your actions changed because of what we learned? If so, how?** Encourage family members to give specific examples of how they've applied learning from the past week.

Share: Today we are going to learn the value of true friendships.

ACTIVITY 1: Friend or Foe?

Point: Choose friends who will encourage your walk with God.

 Supplies: You'll need a Bible

Activity: Open the activity by having someone **read** about the friendship between David and Jonathan. You'll find the key elements of this friendship in 1 Samuel 18:1-4 and 23:16-18. You may want to read these particular passages in advance so as to become more familiar with the story.

When you've shared about David and Jonathan, consider these questions.

- **What do you think made David and Jonathan's friendship successful?** (They both loved God; they encouraged each other; they trusted one another; they didn't let anything come between them; they grew close when facing problems.)

• **What can we learn from this friendship that can help us as believers know who is a true friend?** (True friends look out for each other; true friends encourage; true friends share a love for God.)

Share: I'm going to read a few scenarios or stories. After each, let's talk about whether the person is a true friend or a foe.

Read the following scenarios and allow time for discussion after each one. Use probing questions to draw out your child's reasoning behind his or her decision for each. You may want to alter the characters and stories to match your children's gender. (For example, you could talk about "Joan" instead of "John" in the first scenario.)

SCENARIO ONE: John is a classmate who sits directly across from you in science. You greet each other daily, but haven't really been great friends yet. On one particular occasion, he asks you to join him at the school basketball game. After the game, he invites you to celebrate the victory with his other friends at the local teen hangout. On the way to the restaurant, John's friends pull beers out of a cooler in the back seat and offer them to you and John. John accepts his and looks over at you.

• **What would you do?**
• **Is John a friend or foe?**
• **What else should we know about John before we determine if he is "true friend" material?**
• **Does the fact that John associates with friends who drink bother you? Should it?**

SCENARIO TWO: Your new neighbor, Dan, is as much into computer games as you are. You've been playing games together for a couple of weeks. One day Dan asks if you would make copies of the computer games so he could play at home on his own.
• **What would you do?**
• **Is Dan a friend or foe?**

- What else should we know about Dan before we determine if he is "true friend" material?
- Does the fact that he doesn't seem bothered to illegally copy games bother you? Should it?

SCENARIO THREE: You and your friend Steve are working on a school research project over at Pete's house. After logging on to the Internet, Pete starts surfing for pornography sites. Steve tells him to cut it out—that it's not right—but Pete keeps on surfing. Steve decides to leave and asks you to come along so you don't have to "put up with that kind of thing."

- What would you do?
- Is Steve a friend or foe? What about Pete?
- What else should you know about Steve or Pete before determining whether each is "true friend" material?
- Did Steve do the right thing by leaving (and asking you to come along)?
- Was what Pete did so terrible? Explain.

SCENARIO FOUR: A girl from your youth group, Becky, invites you and several of your friends over for an all-night movie party. Becky has chosen the movies for the evening, and many of them are known to be rather crude.

- What would you do?
- Is Becky a friend or foe?
- What else should you know about Becky before determining whether she's "true friend" material?

 Read aloud James 2:14, 17. Then discuss the following questions with your children.

- **What does this passage tell us about Christians?** (We'll know a Christian by his actions; Christians act in love.)
- **How important is it to choose as your "true friends" people who have Jesus in their hearts?** (Very important: the Bible tells us that we should not enter an "intimate" friendship with a nonbeliever.)
- **Does this mean that you shouldn't associate with people who don't love God? Why or why not?** (No, but there is a difference between associating with and being in a close, intimate friendship with a person.)
- **How does a Christian act out his or her faith in a friendship?** (A friend should always encourage you to do what is right in God's eyes—willing to do what Jesus would do.)

Share: Choosing who will be a true friend isn't always easy. But one thing that can help you as you consider who is a true friend is the actions of that person. Do they honor God? Do they make bad decisions because they don't know any better? Can your friendship with them help them grow? Those who do not know Christ should have different values than you have! Don't get caught in a bad situation—remember the scenarios. The basic test for a healthy relationship are the following questions: Are you being influenced negatively by the relationship? Do you influence the relationship?

Proverbs 27:17 says: As iron sharpens iron, so one friend sharpens another. To find true friends, first you have to be one.

Age Adjustments

YOUNG CHILDREN won't get much out of the scenarios since they're focused on adolescents. But they can enjoy the story of David and Jonathan's friendship. Consider reading that story in one or more children's Bible storybooks and talking about it. Discover together what makes for a good friend.

ACTIVITY 2: Shaping Your Witness

Point: Be courageous in your faith so you can be a strong witness for Christ.

 Supplies: You'll need pipe cleaners and a Bible.

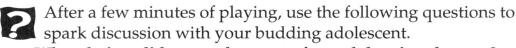

Activity: Give your family members some pipe cleaners and play a simplified game of "Pictionary" by having them shape their pipe cleaners into objects for you to guess. You may want to take turns and give each family member a chance to guess the objects.

After a few minutes of playing, use the following questions to spark discussion with your budding adolescent.

• **What choices did you make as you formed the pipe cleaners?** (I had to choose what to represent; I had to choose which way to bend them and which colors to use.)

• **How is the way you shaped your pipe cleaners like the way you can shape your Christian witness?** (I can choose to be clear with what I say or do; I have to make choices about my witness.)

• **What choices might you have to make to show a friend that you're serious about living life in a Christlike manner?**

(I might have to leave a party; I might have to stand up for my faith if challenged; I might have to tell a friend to stop swearing.)

Read aloud 1 Corinthians 16:13 and **reread** James 2:14, 17. **Share: Think about this thought: If being a Christian were a crime, would there be enough evidence to convict you? We need to be strong in our faith so our friends and peers will know we're serious about our beliefs and so we can confidently make the right decisions—especially when friends might suggest otherwise.**

If you were a Christian as a young teenager, take a few moments to talk about the challenges you faced in living out your faith on a daily basis. Be honest about your successes and failures, and commit to pray for your children as they face inevitable challenges to their faith.

WRAP-UP

Gather everyone in a circle and have family members take turns answering this question: **What's one thing you've learned about God today?**

Next, tell kids you've got a new "Life Verse" you'd like to share with them.

Life Verse: Today's Life Verse is 1 Corinthians 16:13. "Be on your guard; stand firm in the faith; be men of courage; be strong." Have family members repeat the verse two or three times to help them learn it. Then encourage them to practice saying it during the week so they can talk about it at your next family night session.

Close in Prayer: Allow time for each family member to share prayer concerns and answers to prayer. Then close your time together with prayer for each concern. Thank God for listening to and caring about us.

Remember to record your prayer requests so you can refer to them in the future as you see God answering them.

Sidebar:

Family Night

TOOL CHEST

Age Adjustments

YOUNG CHILDREN can enjoy a simpler version of this activity. Give them pipe cleaners and have them shape them into various objects you call out (circle, square, star, etc). Then talk with them about how easy it was to shape the objects, and compare that to how we're to be shaped by God and His Word. Then make a commitment to reading Bible stories with your children daily so they can be shaped by the wisdom in the Bible.

@ 7: Moods

Teaching children that it's normal to experience mood swings during adolescence

Scripture
- Matthew 5:21-22; 6:33
- John 14:17, 26
- 1 Corinthians 2:9-12

ACTIVITY OVERVIEW		
Activity	Summary	Pre-Session Prep
Activity 1: Pressure Points	Learn that mood swings are normal, and discover how to control attitudes.	You'll need aluminum foil and a Bible.
Activity 2: Herding Moods	Learn how seeking God's will can help herd mood swings.	You'll need balloons, a broom, a fan, and a Bible.

Main Points
—Expect mood swings, but learn to control your attitude.
—Seek God's will, and you will learn to herd swinging moods.

LIFE VERSE: "But seek first his kingdom and his righteousness, and all these things will be given to you as well" (Matt. 6:33).

Make it your own
In the space provided below, outline the flow and add any additional ideas
to guide you through the process of conducting this family night.

Prayer & Praise Items
In the space provided below, list any items you wish to pray about or give
praise for during this family night session.

Journal
In the space provided below, capture a record of any fun or meaningful
things which happened during this family night session.

Session Tip

We intentionally have provided more material than we would expect to be used in a single "Family Night" session. You know your family's unique interests and life circumstances best, so feel free to adapt this lesson to meet your family members' needs. Remember, short and simple is better than long and comprehensive.

WARM-UP

Open with Prayer: Begin by having a family member pray, asking God to help everyone in the family understand more about Him through this time. After prayer, review your last lesson by asking these questions:

- **What did we learn about in our last lesson?**
- **What was the life verse?**
- **Have your actions changed because of what we learned? If so, how?** Encourage family members to give specific examples of how they've applied learning from the past week.

Share: Today we are going to learn that mood swings are normal and that one can balance those mood swings.

ACTIVITY 1: Pressure Points

Point: Expect mood swings, yet control your attitude.

Supplies: You'll need aluminum foil and a Bible.

Activity: Give each family member a few sheets of aluminum foil. Explain that they're to shape the foil into one or more familiar objects or creatures (such as dog, elephant, bug, tree, house, or any other items). Allow plenty of time for family members to work with their foil, and encourage creativity and fun.

When family members have finished their sculpting, have them present their objects for the rest of the family to guess. Affirm the creativity expressed, and display items in the center of your table.

 Then discuss the following questions.

- **How easy or difficult was it to work with the foil?** (It was easy and fun to shape; I had a hard time making my item.)
- **What makes the foil easier to work with than, say, paper or cardboard?** (It bends easier; it responds to pressure.)
- **How is the way the foil reacts to pressure like the way you**

might react to outside pressures in life? (I might be easily swayed; it's easy to be shaped by things around us.)

Share: During adolescence, you'll feel a variety of inside and outside pressures, each attempting to shape you in ways you may or may not expect. As your body grows, inside pressures come from high hormone levels needed for growth. Those levels often throw your emotions out of balance, causing you to feel sad, good, happy, angry, and even depressed at times. There are also outside pressures that impact your moods.

Have family members list the kinds of outside pressures that could impact moodiness. Here are a few examples:
- Lack of sleep
- Hunger
- Physical changes
- Circumstances
- The changing moods of others

Then have family members take turns completing the following sentences for each other family member: (name) feels happiest when . . . (name) feels saddest when . . .

  Compare and talk about your responses. Then **read** aloud Matthew 5:21-22. Consider the following questions.
- **What do these verses tell us about anger?** (It's a dangerous emotion; if you're angry with someone and don't deal with it right, you're sinning.)
- **Based on these verses, why do you think it's important to control moods?** (So we don't sin; so we don't hurt anyone.)

Share: The message of these verses is rather strong, but the message is really quite simple: it's important to learn to control our moods so they don't lead us to do wrong things, which can result in violence, emotional or relational hurt, or even spiritual misunderstandings.

Have family members share ideas on how they can help control their mood swings. Some suggestions might include:
- Count to 10 (or 20 or more) before responding to a situation
- Pray for God's help
- Talk with a trusted friend

- Know that it's normal to have wide mood swings
- Focus on God's love so you can withstand the pressures

Share: With God's help, we can lean to control our attitudes—even when hormones and external pressures cause wide mood swings.

ACTIVITY 2: Herding Moods

Point: Seek God's will and learn not to follow your emotions.

 Supplies: You'll need balloons, a broom, a fan, and a Bible

Activity: Blow up 10 to 15 balloons and set them on the floor in a large room. Place a fan (an oscillating fan works best) on a chair so that it blows over the top of the balloons, near an open area or hall where kids will try to herd the balloons. Turn on the fan, and have family members take turns using the broom (or their hands, while not grabbing the balloons) to herd the balloons over to the designated area. To make the game even more challenging, tell participants they may only use the stick-end of the broom to herd the balloons.

Repeat this game as many times as you like so each family member gets at least one turn. You might want to time each attempt so you can see if kids improve on a second or third turn.

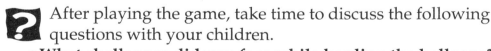

Age Adjustments

YOUNG CHILDREN enjoy playing with aluminum foil. During your discussion with older children, encourage the younger to continue making or playing with objects. There are many lessons you can draw from such an activity: everything from "God gave us a gift of creativity" to "Just as we've shaped these items, God shapes us when we willingly trust in Him."

After playing the game, take time to discuss the following questions with your children.

- **What challenges did you face while herding the balloons?** (They kept scattering; they wouldn't go the way I wanted.)
- **How is this like the way you feel sometimes as you head into adolescence?** (I can't always get things going in the right direction; it's hard to keep emotions in line sometimes.)

Share: It's tough to know how to keep moods and emotions in line as we become teenagers. Often it is especial-

ly hard to understand God's will over our emotions. But the best steps for keeping things in order is to ask God for help and to count on His Holy Spirit to guide us.

  Have volunteers **read** aloud the Scripture passages below. Then discuss the questions that follow.

- John 14:17
- 1 Corinthians 2:9-12
- John 14:26

Age Adjustments

YOUNG CHILDREN will enjoy playing the balloon herding game. After playing, you can talk with younger children about how they felt while herding the balloons. Most will say it was pretty difficult. You can use this teachable moment to help young children see that following God isn't always easy, and it sometimes feels as impossible as herding the balloons. Reassure children, however, that God's Holy Spirit can help to "blow the balloons in the right direction."

- **What do these passages teach us about the Holy Spirit?** (The Holy Spirit lives inside believers; the Holy Spirit can lead us to truth; the Holy Spirit reveals truth; the Holy Spirit can direct us.)
- **How do we hear from the Holy Spirit?** (When we read the Bible; when we listen to other Christians; through our conscience.)

Share: God's Holy Spirit speaks to us first and foremost through the Bible. He also uses other Christians. When we listen to the Holy Spirit and seek advice from parents, godly friends, and teachers, we can discover God's will and overcome the confusing and difficult moods.

WRAP-UP

Gather everyone in a circle and have family members take turns answering this question: **What's one thing you've learned about God today?**

Next, tell kids you've got a new "Life Verse" you'd like to share with them.

Life Verse: Today's Life Verse is Matthew 6:33. "But seek first his kingdom and his righteousness, and all these things will be given to you as well." Have family members repeat the verse to help them learn it. Then encourage them to practice saying it in preparation for the next family night session.

Close in Prayer: Allow for each family member to share concerns and answers to prayer. Then close with prayer for each concern. Thank God for listening to and caring for you. Remember to record prayer requests so you can refer to them in the future.

@ 8: Responsibility

Teaching children that greater freedom requires greater responsibility

Scripture
- Luke 16:10
- Hebrews 13:7
- 2 Peter 3:18
- Ecclesiastes 4:9-12
- 1 Timothy 3:1-7

ACTIVITY OVERVIEW		
Activity	Summary	Pre-Session Prep
Activity 1: Boundaries	Learn that greater freedom requires greater responsibility.	You'll need a shoebox, a flat plate, a golf ball, and a Bible.
Activity 2: Learning to Fly	Learn how mentors can help them make good decisions in life.	You'll need balsa wood air-planes, small Post-It Notes, and a Bible.

Main Points

—Greater freedom requires greater responsibility.

—Mentors can help us navigate through life's difficult situations.

LIFE VERSE: "Whoever can be trusted with very little can also be trusted with much, and whoever is dishonest with very little will also be dishonest with much" Luke 16:10.

Make it your own
In the space provided below, outline the flow and add any additional ideas to guide you through the process of conducting this family night.

Prayer & Praise Items
In the space provided below, list any items you wish to pray about or give praise for during this family night session.

Journal
In the space provided below, capture a record of any fun or meaningful things which happened during this family night session.

Session Tip

We intentionally have provided more material than we would expect to be used in a single "Family Night" session. You know your family's unique interests and life circumstances best, so feel free to adapt this lesson to meet your family members' needs. Remember, short and simple is better than long and comprehensive.

WARM-UP

Open with Prayer: Begin by having a family member pray, asking God to help everyone in the family understand more about Him through this time. After prayer, review your last lesson by asking these questions:

- **What did we learn in our last lesson?**
- **What was the life verse?**
- **Have your actions changed because of what we learned? If so, how?** Encourage family members to give specific examples of how they've applied learning from the past week.

Share: Today we are going to learn how to be responsible.

ACTIVITY 1: Boundaries

Point: Greater freedom requires greater responsibility.

Supplies: You'll need a shoebox, a flat plate, a golf ball, and a Bible

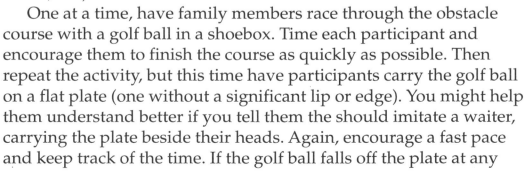

Activity: Create a rather difficult obstacle course for participants to run (over chairs and under tables, etc.).

One at a time, have family members race through the obstacle course with a golf ball in a shoebox. Time each participant and encourage them to finish the course as quickly as possible. Then repeat the activity, but this time have participants carry the golf ball on a flat plate (one without a significant lip or edge). You might help them understand better if you tell them the should imitate a waiter, carrying the plate beside their heads. Again, encourage a fast pace and keep track of the time. If the golf ball falls off the plate at any

time, have the person start the race over again. It is possible that some people won't be able to complete the race using the plate. That's okay.

 After each person has raced with both the shoebox and plate, form a circle and discuss the following questions.
- **What made the plate harder?** (There were no edges/boundaries.)
- **What was it like to race with the golf ball in the shoebox?** (It was easy; I could go real fast.)
- **What was it like to race with the golf ball on the plate?** (It was tough; I had to slow down; I had to watch the ball more.)

Share: When you raced with the shoebox, you had plenty of boundaries to keep the ball in place. But when you raced with the plate, you had fewer boundaries, so you had to slow down and be more careful. The same is true as you grow into adolescence. While you are young, you have plenty of boundaries that are established by parents and teachers. As you grow older, you have fewer boundaries and more freedom. But with more freedom (less boundaries and rules) comes more responsibility, which requires self-discipline as you create your own boundaries to handle the additional responsibilities. Sometimes you even have to slow down and move carefully in life (just as in this game).

Have children list a number of new freedoms they'll have as they grow up. Then choose one and have children talk about the responsibilities that would come with that freedom. Here's an example based on getting a driver's license.
- Freedom: Ability to go where you want without requiring a ride from Mom or Dad.
- Responsibilities: Careful driving to avoid hurting people or breaking the law; upkeep of the car; paying the insurance or car payment.

 Read Luke 16:10, and consider the following questions.
- **What point do you think Jesus is making in this passage?** (Responsibility includes taking care of little things; if you're not responsible with the easy things, you don't get harder things.)
- **What are some of the small responsibilities in your life?** (Taking care of chores; cleaning my room; feeding the cat; doing well in school.)

Help your older children come up with (1) a list of privileges they might gain as they grow older, (2) the responsibilities associated with those privileges, and (3) appropriate consequences for violation of those responsibilities. Discuss these together, and agree on the boundaries; but let your children know that you'll have the final word on whether or not they earn the privileges as they get older.

Share: Boundaries set by Mom and Dad are to teach you self-discipline. Self-discipline is the success element required for you to handle freedom. But as the Bible teaches, with greater freedom comes greater responsibility.

ACTIVITY 2: Learning to Fly

Point: Mentors can help us navigate through life's difficult situations.

 Supplies: You'll need balsa wood airplanes, small sticky notes, and a Bible

Activity: For this activity, you'll need a supply of balsa wood airplanes—the kind that come in those simple paper wraps. Look for them in any hobby store (and many toy stores too). Work with your children to build the planes; then help them carefully push a straight pin in the bottom of the plane near the nose. (Slipping a rubber band over this pin will allow children to fly their planes quickly by stretching the plane back and letting it fly.)

When the planes are complete, have children take turns flying theirs as straight and far as possible. Then explain how attaching small sticky notes to various areas on the wings or tail can change the direction of the flight. Experiment together by attaching one or more note to the wings and tail and sailing the planes across the room. Note how the placement of the sticky notes affects flight. (You may need to cut the sticky notes down to fit the tail section of the plane.)

To add a fun challenge to this activity, set a target (such as a sheet of paper) somewhere in the room and have your pilots attempt to hit it.

 After you've enjoyed plenty of flying time, consider the following questions.

Age Adjustments

AFTER YOUNG CHILDREN participate in the golf ball game, use the discussion time to help them see the reason for their boundaries. Let them know that because you love them, you set appropriate limits on their actions and behaviors. Assure them that they'll get new freedoms as they grow up, but not until they're ready to handle them. If you repeat this activity when younger children are finally approaching adolescence, they'll really catch on to the message as they remember what you taught them when they were younger, applying it to what they are discovering.

• **What was it like flying the planes without the sticky notes?** (They mostly went straight; I could tell which way they were going.)
• **How did you affect the flight with the sticky notes?** (I could control the direction of the plane; I could make the plane fly higher or lower.)

Share: If you watch a big jet's wings in flight—and especially around takeoff and landing—you'll notice subtle (and sometime extreme) changes to portions of the wing. The moving sections of the wings are called ailerons. Ailerons adjust to allow the plane to fly straight or make a safe landing. A mentor in life can be like an aileron. He or she can suggest minor (and major) changes that will help us fly smoothly through life. In the Bible, we learn that Barnabas was Paul's mentor, and Paul was Timothy's mentor.

 Have someone **read** aloud Hebrews 13:7; 2 Peter 3:18; Ecclesiastes 4:9-12; and 1 Timothy 3:1-7. Then consider the following questions.
• **What can we learn about the value of mentors from these passages?** (Mentors can teach us; we learn about trusting God from mentors; it's important to grow daily; two people can do things better than one.)
• **According to the passage in 2 Timothy, what are the qualities of a good mentor?** (A person of integrity; someone who's faithful; someone with self-control; someone who is wise; someone who is respected; someone who is hospitable; someone who can teach.)

Take a few moments to consider who might be good mentors for your older children. If they're involved in a youth group, an adult leader might make a good mentor. While parents must mentor their children, there is added benefit to having someone outside your family also contribute to your child's life by being a mentor. Talk with your church's youth director to get some ideas.

Share: Because they've been there before, mentors can help us navigate through the tough situations in life.

Age Adjustments

YOUNG CHILDREN can get the most out of this activity if you simplify the lesson learned. Explain that, just as the papers helped the planes to fly, teachers and parents can help you fly straight (or do the right thing) in life.

Their wisdom and experience are invaluable as we grow older and as we attempt to grow closer to God.

WRAP-UP

Gather everyone in a circle and have family members take turns answering this question: **What's one thing you've learned about God today?**

Next, tell kids you've got a new "Life Verse" you'd like to share with them.

Life Verse: Today's Life Verse is Luke 16:10. "Whoever can be trusted with very little can also be trusted with much, and whoever is dishonest with very little will also be dishonest with much." Have family members repeat the verse two or three times to help them learn it. Then encourage them to practice saying it during the week so they can talk about it at your next family night session.

Close in Prayer: Allow time for each family member to share prayer concerns and answers to prayer. Then close your time together with prayer for each concern. Thank God for listening to and caring about us.

Remember to record your prayer requests so you can refer to them in the future as you see God answering them.

© 9: The Value of Values

Teaching children how the world's values compare to God's values

Scripture
- Matthew 5:3-12
- Proverbs 1:3-4

ACTIVITY OVERVIEW		
Activity	**Summary**	**Pre-Session Prep**
Activity 1: Left Is Right, Right?	Learn that God's values are different from the world's.	You'll need table settings and a Bible.
Activity 2: Applied Principles	Learn the value of applying wisdom.	You'll need a 2X4, a brick or other pieces of wood, and a Bible.

Main Points

—God's view of righteous living is not the same as the world's view of successful living.

—When we apply God's Word to our lives, we can live according to God's values.

LIFE VERSE: "For acquiring a disciplined and prudent life, doing what is right and just and fair; for giving prudence to the simple, knowledge and discretion to the young" (Prov. 1:3-4).

Make it your own
In the space provided below, outline the flow and add any additional ideas to guide you through the process of conducting this family night.

Prayer & Praise Items
In the space provided below, list any items you wish to pray about or give praise for during this family night session.

Journal
In the space provided below, capture a record of any fun or meaningful things which happened during this family night session.

Session Tip

We intentionally have provided more material than we would expect to be used in a single "Family Night" session. You know your family's unique interests and life circumstances best, so feel free to adapt this lesson to meet your family members' needs. Remember, short and simple is better than long and comprehensive.

 ### WARM-UP

Open with Prayer: Begin by having a family member pray, asking God to help everyone in the family understand more about Him through this time. After prayer, review your last lesson by asking these questions:

- **What did we learn from our last lesson?**
- **What was the life verse?**
- **Have your actions changed because of what we learned? If so, how?** Encourage family members to give specific examples of how they've applied learning from the past week.

Share: Today we are going to learn how God's values differ from the world's.

ACTIVITY 1: Left Is Right, Right?

Point: God's view of righteous living is not the same as the world's view of successful living.

Supplies: You'll need table settings and a Bible

Activity: Set the table with two settings for each person placed closely together (with a cup on a saucer in the middle, a spoon on the left, and a fork on the right at each setting). Have family members sit at the table with the two settings in front of them. Explain that you're going to give instructions for them to follow using the silverware, but that the instructions will be the opposite of what they should do. For example, if you say to pick up something from the right setting, they're to pick up something from

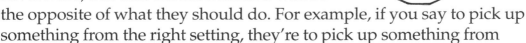

the left instead. When they understand the rules, read the following quickly to see if kids can keep up.

Share: Using your right hand, pick up the fork on the right and place it next to the fork on the left. Then using your left hand, pick up the cup on the right and place it next to the spoon on the left. Using the same hand, now pick up the fork on the left, next to the plate, and put it next to the spoon on the right. Now using your right hand, pick up the plate on the right and place it on top of the cup on the far left. With your left hand, take the cup on the right and place it on top of the saucer on your left. Finally using your right hand, pick up the spoon on the left and place it in the cup on the right.

If they actually were able to follow the instructions exactly, the final setting should include a saucer with a cup on it, the second saucer on top of the cup, the second cup stacked on the second saucer, and a spoon in the second cup. But don't worry if kids can't keep up. They'll enjoy the challenge and learn from the difficulty of the activity anyway. When family members have attempted this challenge (perhaps more than once if they desire), consider the following questions.

- **What were your reactions as I read the instructions?** (I couldn't keep up; I got confused.)
- **What made this a difficult activity?** (We did everything backward; we had to think in a way that wasn't normal.)

Share: If I had given you instructions that weren't reversed, you probably could have kept up and completed the task a lot easier. It's a challenge to do things that don't feel natural. The same is true in life. The values that the world believes in are easy to follow (and presented by TV, music, and movies every day). But God calls us to follow His ways, which may seem unnatural at first (just as we felt in this activity).

Have someone list the qualities of a successful person, according to the world's values. (They might choose a movie star, a successful businessperson, or a sports star.) Some values might include: intelligence, confidence, ability to control others, power, money, and so on. Then have someone **read** aloud Matthew 5:3-12 and list the values described in this passage. Some examples might include:

patience; mercy; peacemaking; gentleness; and pure hearts.

- **What would the world look like if people sought the qualities listed in Matthew rather than worldly qualities?** (People would be nicer to each other; no one would be without food; people would look for ways to help each other; there would be no war.)

Share: Our natural desires are for the things of this world: power, money, and pleasure. But we need to be concerned about what brings glory to God, instead of fulfilling our selfish desires. Since it is not natural, as in this game, we must train ourselves to be godly.

ACTIVITY 2: Applied Principles

Point: When we apply God's Word to our lives, we can live according to God's values.

 Supplies: You'll need a 2X4, a brick or blocks of wood, and a Bible

Activity: Set a brick (or a 2X4 block) in the middle of a room. (You could also do this activity outdoors if you prefer.) Set a 2X4 atop the brick (it's okay if it isn't balanced). Have family members gather around as you explain the activity.

Share: The object of this activity is to have a lighter person lift a heavier person across this home-made teeter-totter. But the trick is that you'll have to determine before you step onto the board where each person will stand. I'm going to give you a principle of physics that you can apply as you consider how to do this activity.

Explain that the law of leverage works this way: Weight times the distance from the fulcrum (or brick, in this case) on the side with the

Age Adjustments

YOUNG CHILDREN will probably get frustrated if you attempt this activity as-is. You may simplify it by using colored blocks and assigning wrong colors to each block, having children stack them in certain ways. For example, you might call the blue block green, the green block yellow, and the yellow block blue. After giving a series of instructions for stacking, talk about how difficult it was to follow the instructions. Then instead of applying the message of values (which may be too difficult for children to comprehend), help children see how this activity is like trying to do the right thing when you don't know what the right thing is. Repeat the activity with proper colors and talk about how reading the Bible and learning in church can help "sort out the colors" and make our decisions easier.

lighter person must be greater than the weight times the distance from the fulcrum on the side with the heavier person in order to lift that person. Here's an example of how this works (explain this to your family as they try to work out the details). The person being lifted is Dad, who weighs about 200 pounds. The child who will lift him weighs about 100 pounds. In order for the child to lift the dad, he'll have to be twice the distance (or more) from the fulcrum as his dad. (The weight of 200 times 2 feet equals 400, and the weight of 100 times 4 feet is also 400; so the minimum distance is four feet if the Dad is two feet from the fulcrum.)

Help family members with the calculations, and then have them step onto the board to see how leverage works. You may want to try this activity with a variety of participants on either side.

 After a few lifts, consider the following questions.

- **How was the information I provided helpful?** (It told us what we needed to do to succeed; we used it and accomplished the goal.)
- **How is applying this principle like applying wisdom in our lives?** (If we apply wisdom, we can do great things; wisdom helps us to accomplish things we didn't think we could do.)

  Have someone **read** aloud Proverbs 1:3-4. Then consider these questions.

- **What does this passage tell us about the value of wisdom?** (We can learn to be clever; we can make good choices; we can live with discipline.)
- **What are some ways to acquire wisdom?** (Study the Bible; listen to parents and the pastor at church; talk with mentors or other godly people; pray.)

Share: When we apply God's principles to our lives, we gain wisdom that will allow us to avoid many problems and pain. God's Word is full of wisdom we can use each day that will help us grow closer to Him and live in ways that are pleasing to Him.

Age Adjustments

YOUNG CHILDREN can play with the materials in this activity in a different way. Instead of attempting to teach the importance of applying principles, simply enjoy some makeshift teeter-totter time with your younger children. Then you can use this moment to teach about any of a number of topics (including: "sometimes we feel happy or up, sometimes sad or down; but up or down, we can trust God"; or "a teeter-totter is pretty boring with one person, but lots of fun with two—that's why it's good to make friends").

WRAP-UP

Gather everyone in a circle, and have family members take turns answering this question: **What's one thing you've learned about God today?**

Next, tell kids you have a new "Life Verse" you'd like to share with them.

Life Verses: Today's Life Verses are Proverbs 1:3-4. "For acquiring a disciplined and prudent life, doing what is right and just and fair; for giving prudence to the simple, knowledge and discretion to the young." Have family members repeat the verses two or three times to help them learn them. Then encourage them to practice saying them during the week so they can talk about them at your next family night session.

Close in Prayer: Allow time for each family member to share prayer concerns and answers to prayer. Then close your time together with prayer for each concern. Thank God for listening to and caring about us.

Remember to record your prayer requests so you can refer to them in the future as you see God answering them.

@ 10: Peer Pressure

Teaching children the importance of having confidence to do what's right when peers recommend wrong choices

Scripture
- 2 Corinthians 6:14-18
- Proverbs 13:20; 18:24
- Hebrews 5:14

ACTIVITY OVERVIEW		
Activity	Summary	Pre-Session Prep
Activity 1: Surrounded	Learn how surrounding yourself with godly friends can help fight negative peer pressure.	You'll need pennies, nickels, a dime, masking tape, a table, and a Bible.
Activity 2: Planning Ahead	Learn how to avoid making wrong decisions under pressure.	You'll need three different colors of paper, three buckets, and a Bible.

Main Points

—When we surround ourselves with godly friends, we can stand up to negative peer pressure.

—Know ahead of time how you might respond, and you can avoid making wrong decisions under pressure.

LIFE VERSE: "But solid food is for the mature, who by constant use have trained themselves to distinguish good from evil" (Heb. 5:14).

Make it your own
In the space provided below, outline the flow and add any additional ideas to guide you through the process of conducting this family night.

Prayer & Praise Items
In the space provided below, list any items you wish to pray about or give praise for during this family night session.

Journal
In the space provided below, capture a record of any fun or meaningful things which happened during this family night session.

Session Tip

We intentionally have provided more material than we would expect to be used in a single "Family Night" session. You know your family's unique interests and life circumstances best, so feel free to adapt this lesson to meet your family members' needs. Remember, short and simple is better than long and comprehensive.

WARM-UP

Open with Prayer: Begin by having a family member pray, asking God to help everyone in the family understand more about Him through this time. After prayer, review your last lesson by asking these questions:

- **What did we learn in our last lesson?**
- **What was the life verse?**
- **Have your actions changed because of what we learned? If so, how?** Encourage family members to give specific examples of how they've applied learning from the past week.

Share: Today we are going to learn how to stand up to negative peer pressure.

ACTIVITY 1: Surrounded

Point: When we surround ourselves with godly friends, we can stand up to negative peer pressure.

 Supplies: You'll need pennies, nickels, a dime, masking tape, a table, and a Bible.

Activity: Before you begin, you'll need to create a "playing field" on a table with a slick surface. (Don't choose a table that will mar easily, as coins will be scooted across it during the activity.)

Use strips of masking tape to mark a "field" about 18 inches wide across the width of the table. Place the dime in the middle of the field. Place the nickels for each team behind the tape line—all shots must start from behind the tape. Form two teams and have them stand on opposite sides of the playing field. (A team can be one

person). Set a nickel in front of each team, near the edge of the table. Then explain the rules for the game.

Share: We're going to play a game to see who can knock the dime across the opposing team's goal (the end of the table). Alternating turns, each team must flick the nickel toward the dime to see if they can knock it off the table. One point will be awarded each time a team knocks the dime off the opposing team's table edge. After each flick, you must retrieve your nickel and wait for your next turn. The dime cannot be touched by any player during the game (unless, of course, it falls to the floor and must be placed in the middle of the table again).

Play a few rounds, and see if anyone can knock off the dime. It will be difficult but possible. Then change the game a bit by placing a barrier of pennies (at least 25) around the dime. Start the game again and watch as kids try to knock the dime off the table. This time, the challenge will be much greater as the pennies will block their attempts to hit the dime. After you've played this version of the game awhile, consider the following questions.

- **What was it like to knock the dime off during the first rounds?** (It was hard; we could do it pretty easily when we aimed; it wasn't too tough.)
- **What changed when I placed the pennies around the dime?** (It was much harder to knock the dime off; we couldn't get through the pennies.)
- **If you were the dime, which version of the game would you prefer?** (The second, because I'd be safer; the second, because I wouldn't get hit as much.)

Read aloud Proverbs 13:20; Proverbs 18:24; and 2 Corinthians 6:14-18. Then discuss the following questions.

- **What do these verses tell us about friends?** (Godly friends are good for us; friends love you in good and bad times; don't team up with nonbelievers.)
- **How is surrounding yourself with godly friends like placing a penny barrier around the dime?** (Godly friends protect you; you can't get hurt as much if you have good friends around you.)

Share: Not all peer pressure is bad. If the pressure is to stay

away from drugs, that's good peer pressure. But if the pressure is to do something you know is wrong, that's negative peer pressure. When we're on our own and facing negative peer pressure, we're kind of like the dime in the first round of this game. It's much easier to be moved by someone who wants to pressure us. But when we surround ourselves with godly friends, we're like the dime in the second round of the game—we're less likely to be moved.

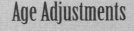

 Consider the following question.
- **What kinds of things can godly friends do to help us face negative peer pressure?** (They can encourage us; they can hold us accountable; they can remind us what the Bible says.)

1 Kings 12:1-17

Share: Surrounding yourself with godly friends gives you confidence to face difficult situations.

II Kings 13:1-33

ACTIVITY 2: Planning Ahead

Point: Know ahead of time how you might respond, and you can avoid making wrong decisions under pressure.

 Supplies: You'll need three different colors of paper, three buckets, and a Bible.

Activity: Tape a different colored sheet of paper to each of three buckets (trash cans work nicely). Then crumple up a bunch of the same colored paper (equal numbers of each) and set these paper balls on a table a few feet from the buckets.

Invite family members to take turns playing this game. Have the participant kneel near the buckets. Explain that the object of the game is to catch as many paper wads as possible and place them in the coordinating buckets. They'll receive one point for each correctly placed paper wad.

Begin the game by tossing the wads at a fast pace. Vary your tossing pace to stay just ahead of the person catching, so he or she will

Age Adjustments

YOUNG CHILDREN can play a version of this game with checkers if the coins are too small for them to knock around. Place a chess piece or a specially marked checker in the middle of the table, and play the game as described in the activity. After having children play both rounds (with the checker on its own and with it surrounded), talk about peer pressure in age-appropriate terms. Younger children may not face the pressure to try drugs or alcohol, but some may feel pressured to cheat, steal, or say mean things about a classmate. This can be a great learning activity for children; and kids are never too young to learn the value of building great, godly friendships.

miss one out of three. Halfway through the game, tell the participant that each paper wad in a wrong-color bucket will be worth five points. Add up the score at the end (one point for matching paper wads, five points for each non-matching paper wad).

Explain that you're going to repeat the game, with the very same rules. Then begin tossing papers again. It's probable that your child will intentionally put wrong-colored papers in the buckets. That's the way to score the most points . . . and the best lesson can come from such a decision. If the child repeats the same actions as the first time, play again until he or she "gets it" and starts putting papers in non-matching buckets. (It's okay to give a hint if your child doesn't figure it out right away.)

Once again, tally the score. Then compare the score to previous attempts. After plenty of fun playing the game, consider the following questions.

- **What was it like to play this game?** (It was hard; I had to think quickly; I had to be alert.)
- **How did the game change the second time you played?** (I knew what to do to get more points; I knew all the rules at the beginning.)

Share: Just as it may have been difficult to adjust to a rule change in the middle of the game, it's tough to make decisions in the middle of situations. During the second round, however, you knew ahead of time what you'd be doing to score the most points. This is an advantage in real life too. Knowing ahead of time what you might do in any given situation helps you to make a better decision once you're facing that situation.

Read Hebrews 5:14 and discuss how we grow and mature as Christians. Explain that we grow when we train ourselves to look at situations from God's perspective and determine whether the actions honor Him or not.

Consider the following questions.
- **How can you plan ahead of time to make good decisions and avoid negative pressures?** (Pray for God's help; trust the Holy Spirit to guide us; know the Bible and memorize important verses; stay away from situations that could lead to negative peer pressure; be confident in what we believe.)

• **How can we (as your parents) help you to plan well for such situations?** (Tell us what you know or have experienced; pray for us; help us see what dangers lie ahead.)

Have children share "what if?" scenarios to explore how they might respond to pressure situations. Offer your guidance and lead children to appropriate scripture passages as you work through these possibilities together. Some scenarios might include: a peer offers a cigarette; someone says, "I have the answers to tomorrow's quiz!"; a friend invites your child to join him in viewing pornographic web sites.

WRAP-UP

Gather everyone in a circle and have family members take turns answering this question: **What's one thing you've learned about God today?**

Next, tell kids you've got a new "Life Verse" you'd like to share with them.

Age Adjustments

YOUNG CHILDREN **can certainly participate in this activity by tossing the wadded up paper. But they probably won't get as much out of the lesson portion of this activity as they will in the first activity in this lesson. Simply allow them to enjoy throwing paper around and enjoy the laughter together. Sometimes, just spending time having fun (especially "messy" fun) can be a great family-builder for younger children.**

Life Verse: Today's Life Verse is Hebrews 5:14. "But solid food is for the mature, who by constant use have trained themselves to distinguish good from evil." Have family members repeat the verse two or three times to help them learn it. Then encourage them to practice saying it during the week so they can talk about it at your next family night session.

Close in Prayer: Allow time for each family member to share prayer concerns and answers to prayer. Then close your time together with prayer for each concern. Thank God for listening to and caring about us.

Remember to record your prayer requests so you can refer to them in the future as you see God answering them.

11: Getting Along With Parents

Teaching children the importance of their relationship with parents

Scripture
- Proverbs 4:1-9; 6:20-23
- Psalm 103:13
- Deuteronomy 6:47
- Ephesians 6:1-4

ACTIVITY OVERVIEW		
Activity	Summary	Pre-Session Prep
Activity 1: Communication Is a Two-Way Street	Learn the importance of open and clear communication.	You'll need paper and a Bible.
Activity 2: Working Together	Learn to obey parents and that parents shouldn't exasperate children.	You'll need rope, tape, candy, and a Bible.

Main Points
—Open communication is vital to healthy relationships and beneficial to children and parents.

—When parents avoid exasperating children, they're free to raise them in the instruction of the Lord.

LIFE VERSE: "'Honor your father and mother'—which is the first commandment with a promise—that it may go well with you and that you may enjoy long life on the earth" (Eph. 6:2-3).

Make it your own

In the space provided below, outline the flow and add any additional ideas to guide you through the process of conducting this family night.

Prayer & Praise Items

In the space provided below, list any items you wish to pray about or give praise for during this family night session.

Journal

In the space provided below, capture a record of any fun or meaningful things which happened during this family night session.

Session Tip

We intentionally have provided more material than we would expect to be used in a single "Family Night" session. You know your family's unique interests and life circumstances best, so feel free to adapt this lesson to meet your family members' needs. Remember, short and simple is better than long and comprehensive.

WARM-UP

Open with Prayer: Begin by having a family member pray, asking God to help everyone in the family understand more about Him through this time. After prayer, review your last lesson by asking these questions:

• **What did we learn in our last lesson?**
• **What was the life verse?**
• **Have your actions changed because of what we learned? If so, how?** Encourage family members to give specific examples of how they've applied learning from the past week.

Share: Today we are going to learn some tips for getting along with parents.

ACTIVITY 1: Communication Is a Two-Way Street

Point: Open communication is vital to healthy relationships and beneficial to children and parents.

Supplies: You'll need paper and a Bible

Activity: This is an activity you'll want to do one at a time with your children. Have a parent and child stand back to back. Give each a plain sheet of paper. Then have the parent fold and tear the paper, giving instructions to the child to repeat his or her actions. Let the child know that he or she may not ask any questions during this activity. As the parent folds and tears the paper, the child will do his or her best to copy the instructions.

After numerous instructions, have the parent and child unfold their papers and compare them. They'll probably look like snowflakes or Swiss cheese! Note any differences in the unfolded papers. Then repeat the activity with each other child.

When everyone's had a turn to play, try the activity again, but this time allow plenty of interaction between parent and child. Encourage the child to ask clarifying questions if needed. Again, compare the finished papers. Then consider the following questions.

- **What made this activity difficult at first?** (I couldn't ask questions; I didn't know what you were doing with yours.)
- **What made the activity a bit easier the second time?** (I was able to talk; I learned which way you were holding the paper.)
- **How do these two activities illustrate the importance of communication?** (When you don't talk, you can't understand what's going on; people who don't talk get wrong messages; communication is a two-way street.)

Share: As you grow into adolescence, it's not unusual for you to keep to yourself or talk with peers but not parents. Yet, without two-way communication, parents and children often get wrong messages—just as we ended up with different papers in the activity. We both benefit when we talk openly: you learn skills and knowledge that can help you survive the tumultuous teens, and we begin to grow a healthy relationship with our children who are well on their way toward adulthood.

 Consider the following question.
- **What are the elements of good communication?** (Honesty; politeness; managing anger; eye contact; trust; openness.)

With a tennis ball in hand, sit at a table across from your child and try this method of conversation. First explain that the conversation is like a tennis match, where each person passes the ball back and forth. Encourage children to ask open-ended questions (questions that can't be answered with a simple "yes" or "no") and to answer in detail when asked a question. Choose a topic for the conversation such as: "What do your friends talk about?" or "What are some good ways to live out our faith among non-Christians?" Begin the conversation with the first question, and roll the ball across the table. Continue the conversation, rolling the ball with each response, for five minutes. Emphasize that only the person with the ball is allowed to speak.

 Repeat the activity with all children and then **read** aloud Proverbs 4:1-9 and 6:20-23. Then **share: One of the best ways to grow in wisdom is to learn from parents. These verses tell us that obtaining wisdom is the best thing we can do.**

- **Why do you think communication is even more important for parents and children during adolescent years?** (There are more pressures; we're learning how to become adults; the issues we face are tougher.)

Read aloud Psalm 103:13 and Deuteronomy 6:47. Then **share: God has given parents an important role: to help their children discover God's values and offer wisdom to help them make good choices.**

Ask your child to make a commitment to open communication, so that together you can grow wiser and closer through the challenges of adolescence.

Age Adjustments

YOUNG CHILDREN can enjoy a simpler version of the paper tearing activity. Instead of giving folding and tearing instructions, give simple instructions for drawing shapes and have the child attempt to copy them. Work within the ability level of your child as you give instructions and compare finished drawings. For the second round, you can simply show the child what you're drawing and have him or her copy you. The lesson will be similar to the one explored above: "When we talk with and watch our parents, we can learn what they're saying; but when we don't talk with or watch them, we get mixed up sometimes."

ACTIVITY 2: Working Together

Point: When parents avoid exasperating children, they're free to raise them in the instruction of the Lord.

 Supplies: You'll need rope, tape, candy, and a Bible.

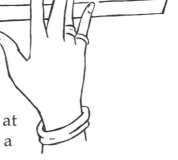

Activity: This activity should be done with children one at a time. If you have more than one adolescent child, you might want to plan on staggering this activity over a couple of nights, doing it with children at different times. Or you can simply have children take turns.

Use soft rope to tie parent and child together at the ankle and corresponding wrist. Allow about a three-foot space between parent and child. Then use the tape to make marks on the floor near their feet. These marks are the "don't cross" lines and should be near the location of each person's feet when the rope is stretched to its maximum distance. Place a bowl of candy on both sides of the tape—just out of reach of either person no matter how much they lean toward it. (The candy should be accessible, however, should the parent or child help the other person lean toward it. Just don't tell them about this idea as you're arranging the candy bowls.)

Tell participants to see if they can get some candy, without crossing the lines. Then watch as they attempt on their own to grab the candy. Disqualify them if they cross the line or attempt to break the rope. Eventually, they may discover the way to win is to help one another. If so, congratulate them for coming up with a great idea. If not, suggest this idea and watch as they enjoy the activity and grab some candy.

 After the activity is over, snack on the candy and discuss the following questions.

- **What was difficult about this activity?** (We couldn't reach the candy; we fought each other for the candy; we both went different directions.)
- **What did you learn was the key to getting the candy?** (Working together; helping each other lean further.)

  Read Ephesians 6:1-4. Then **share: This passage gives good advice for both parents and children.**

- **What does this say to parents?** (Don't discourage children; don't exasperate children; raise children to know Jesus.)
- **What does this say to children?** (Obey parents; honor parents; show respect to parents.)

Talk together about ways you can follow the instruction in this passage. Be honest and share your own struggles with "not exasperating" children. Make a commitment to being as positive and uplifting as possible with your children. And ask your children to make a commitment to respect and obey you. If you both work on these things, you'll discover a wonderful relationship together that can grow for years to come.

Age Adjustments

YOUNG CHILDREN will enjoy the candy activity as much as older children. It's even possible they'll figure out the key to success faster than their older siblings, as they're probably not as quick to go in the opposite direction as parents. After discovering together the power of working together, use this activity to simply teach younger children that "when we work together, we can do great things."

WRAP-UP

Gather everyone in a circle and have family members take turns answering this question: **What's one thing you've learned about God today?**

Next, tell kids you've got a new "Life Verse" you'd like to share with them.

Life Verses: Today's Life Verses are Ephesians 6:2-3. "'Honor your father and mother'—which is the first commandment with a promise—that it may go well with you and that you may enjoy long life on the earth." Have family members repeat the verses two or three times to help them learn them. Then encourage them to practice saying them during the week so they can talk about it at your next family night session.

Close in Prayer: Allow time for each family member to share prayer concerns and answers to prayer. Then close your time together with prayer for each concern. Thank God for listening to and caring about us.

Remember to record your prayer requests so you can refer to them in the future as you see God answering them.

⌾ 12: Identity in Christ

Teaching children that their identity comes from Christ

Scripture
- 2 Corinthians 5:17-20; 6:3-10
- Romans 12:4-5

ACTIVITY OVERVIEW		
Activity	Summary	Pre-Session Prep
Activity 1: Commercial Thoughts	Learn that the world doesn't define who we are.	You'll need paper, pencils, and a Bible.
Activity 2: Writing Feet?	Learn that each person has a unique gift from God.	You'll need pencils, paper, and a Bible.

Main Points

—Our identity is found in Christ, not the world.

—As a member of God's body, you serve a unique and important purpose.

LIFE VERSE: "Therefore, if anyone is in Christ, he is a new creation; the old has gone, the new has come! . . . We are therefore Christ's ambassadors, as though God were making his appeal through us. We implore you on Christ's behalf: Be reconciled to God" (2 Cor. 5:17, 20).

Make it your own
In the space provided below, outline the flow and add any additional ideas to guide you through the process of conducting this family night.

Prayer & Praise Items
In the space provided below, list any items you wish to pray about or give praise for during this family night session.

Journal
In the space provided below, capture a record of any fun or meaningful things which happened during this family night session.

Session Tip

We intentionally have provided more material than we would expect to be used in a single "Family Night" session. You know your family's unique interests and life circumstances best, so feel free to adapt this lesson to meet your family members' needs. Remember, short and simple is better than long and comprehensive.

WARM-UP

Open with Prayer: Begin by having a family member pray, asking God to help everyone in the family understand more about Him through this time. After prayer, review your last lesson by asking these questions:

- **What did we learn about in our last lesson?**
- **What was the life verse?**
- **Have your actions changed because of what we learned? If so, how?** Encourage family members to give specific examples of how they've applied learning from the past week.

Share: Today we are going to learn how we find our identity in Christ.

ACTIVITY 1: Commercial Thoughts

Point: Our identity is found in Christ, not the world.

 Supplies: You'll need paper, pencils, and a Bible

Activity: For this activity, you'll be watching television! And instead of flipping channels to avoid commercials, you'll be flipping to find them. Give each family member a sheet of paper and a pen or pencil. You might also want to have some popcorn handy to enjoy during the activity.

Explain that you'll be watching commercials and answering two questions based on each commercial:

- What is the product being sold?
- What does the product promise to do?

For example, a toothpaste commercial might promise "more boyfriends" or "a life filled with smiles." Encourage family members to think about the hidden promises being made rather than the features of the product. Watch a few commercials together and explain how you'd answer the questions for each, giving family members an idea of what you're looking for. Then start the activity.

Number the commercials as you watch them so it's easier to compare notes after you've finished. Watch up to 10 different commercials; then compare notes on those commercials.

- **What kinds of messages did the commercials give?** (You can have a better life with our product; you are only important if you use our product.)
- **What do commercials tell you about your identity?** (You are only as good as the stuff you own; products make you a better person.)

Share: Television and other media of the world teach us that we get our identity from things (like clothing, music, shoes, and even toothpaste). But the Bible tells us we get out identities elsewhere.

  Read aloud 2 Corinthians 5:17-20. Then consider these questions.

- **What do these verses tell us about our identities?** (We're new creations in Christ; we are Christ's ambassadors.)
- **How are ambassadors like "commercials" for Christ?** (We show the world what's great about Jesus; we tell others that they get their identity in Christ.)

Read 2 Corinthians 6:3-10 and discuss what this passage tells us about representing Christ to the world. These verses tell us that we shouldn't let the situations in the world or the people of the world sway our beliefs. Help your children see that God does not wants us to compromise our beliefs. Then consider these questions.

- **How do people discover what you believe?** (They can tell by what we say; by our actions; by what we stand up for.)
- **How does finding your identity in Christ compare with finding your identity in worldly things?** (Identity in Christ is based on God's love; things the world thinks are important change often; God's love for me never changes.)

Share: God gives us our identity in Christ. We are not better or worse based on the clothes we wear or the music we listen to. God designed us to be His people—and He loves us as we are and with an unchanging love.

ACTIVITY 2: Writing Feet

Point: As a member of God's body, you serve a unique and important purpose.

 Supplies: You'll need pencils, paper, and a Bible.

Activity: Place a large sheet of paper on the floor (a smooth surface is necessary for this activity). Invite one family member to play first, and give him or her a pen or water-based marker to use. Explain that the goal of the activity is to write a simple instruction on the paper for another family member to follow. If the family member understands and completes the instruction, the player wins the game. (Instructions could be anything from "get me a glass of water" to "give Mom a hug.")

Just as your children are thinking "This is easy!" explain that they must write the message with their feet (holding the pen or marker between their toes). Have children remove shoes and play the game. Repeat a few times so each family member gets a chance to participate. Award a prize to those who succeed. Then consider the following questions.

- **What made this activity difficult?** (We had to write with our feet; feet aren't made for writing; it was hard to hold the pen; I couldn't hold my feet steady.)
- **What other actions would be difficult or impossible if we used the wrong body part?** (Walking on our hands is hard; it's impossible to talk with your nose; elbows can't hear.)

Age Adjustments

BECAUSE IT'S RATHER ABSTRACT, YOUNG CHILDREN may not get much out of this activity. To help young children see their identity in Christ, have them create a self-portrait. Then ask children how their picture compares to the way they think God sees them. Help children discover that God sees them as terrific, special people who don't need to wear any particular shoes or have any particular toys to be loved. This can be an extremely affirming (and freeing) message for young children who are influenced all too often by the messages of "worldly identity" on television.

Have fun with this second question, and come up with as many strange scenarios as you can. Then **read** aloud Romans 12:4-5 and discuss the following questions.

- **What do these verses tell us about our role in God's church?** (We each have different roles; some of us are hands and others are feet; each has his or her own unique gifts.)
- **How do Christians work together as "different body parts"?** (We help each other; some are good at teaching and others are good at serving.)

Age Adjustments

YOUNG CHILDREN may want to participate in the foot-writing activity, but you can simplify it if necessary. Consider having them create simple recognizable shapes rather than write instructions. Then make the application that "feet were made for walking" and "hands for writing." Help children see that each person in the family (and in the family of God) may appear to be different, act differently, or have different talents, but all are equally important and valuable to God.

Share: We were all designed to fill a role in God's church body: we each have a part; we each were designed by God for a specific purpose (a spiritual gift). So if one does not do his or her part, the others must cover, just as in the object lesson. What part are you, and what are you doing for the body?

WRAP-UP
Take turns answering this question: **What's one thing you've learned about God today?**

Next, tell kids you've got a new "Life Verse" you'd like to share with them.

Life Verses: Today's Life Verses are 2 Corinthians 5:17, 20. "Therefore, if anyone is in Christ, he is a new creation; the old has gone, the new has come! . . . We are therefore Christ's ambassadors, as though God were making his appeal through us. We implore you on Christ's behalf: Be reconciled to God." Have family members repeat the verse two or three times to help them learn it. Then encourage them to practice saying it during the week so they can talk about it at your next family night session.

Close in Prayer: Allow time for each family member to share prayer concerns and answers to prayer. Then close your time together with prayer for each concern. Thank God for listening to and caring about us.

Remember to record your prayer requests so you can refer to them in the future as you see God answering them.

How to Lead Your Child to Christ

SOME THINGS TO CONSIDER AHEAD OF TIME:

1. Realize that God is more concerned about your child's eternal destiny and happiness than you are. "The Lord is not slow in keeping His promise. . . . He is patient with you, not wanting anyone to perish, but everyone to come to repentance" (2 Peter 3:9).

2. Pray specifically beforehand that God will give you insights and wisdom in dealing with each child on his or her maturity level.

3. Don't use terms like "take Jesus into your heart," "dying and going to hell," and "accepting Christ as your personal Savior." Children are either too literal ("How does Jesus breathe in my heart?") or the words are too clichéd and trite for their understanding.

4. Deal with each child alone, and don't be in a hurry. Make sure he or she understands. Discuss. Take your time.

A FEW CAUTIONS:

1. When drawing children to Himself, Jesus said for others to "allow" them to come to Him (see Mark 10:14). Only with adults did He use the term "compel" (see Luke 14:23). Do not compel children.

2. Remember that unless the Holy Spirit is speaking to the child, there will be no genuine heart experience of regeneration. Parents, don't get caught up in the idea that Jesus will return the day before you were going to speak to your child about salvation and that it will be too late. Look at God's character— He *is* love! He is not dangling your child's soul over hell. Wait on God's timing.

    Pray with faith, believing. Be concerned, but don't push.

THE PLAN:

1. **God loves you.** Recite John 3:16 with your child's name in place of "the world."

2. **Show the child his or her need of a Savior.**

   a. Deal with sin carefully. There is one thing that cannot enter heaven—sin.

   b. Be sure your child knows what sin is. Ask him to name some (things common to children—lying, sassing, disobeying, etc.). Sin is doing or thinking anything wrong according to God's Word. It is breaking God's Law.

   c. Ask the question "Have you sinned?" If the answer is no, do not continue. Urge him to come and talk to you again when he does feel that he has sinned. Dismiss him. You may want to have prayer first, however, thanking God "for this young child who is willing to do what is right." Make it easy for him to talk to you again, but do not continue. Do not say, "Oh, yes, you have too sinned!" and then name some. With children, wait for God's conviction.

   d. If the answer is yes, continue. He may even give a personal illustration of some sin he has done recently or one that has bothered him.

   e. Tell him what God says about sin: We've all sinned ("There is no one righteous, not even one," Rom. 3:10). And because of that sin, we can't get to God ("For the wages of sin is death," Rom. 6:23). So He had to come to us ("but the gift of God is eternal life in Christ Jesus our Lord," Rom. 6:23).

   f. Relate God's gift of salvation to Christmas gifts—we don't earn them or pay for them; we just accept them and are thankful for them.

3. **Bring the child to a definite decision.**

   a. Christ must be received if salvation is to be possessed.

   b. Remember, do not force a decision.

   c. Ask the child to pray out loud in her own words. Give her some things she could say if she seems unsure. Now be prepared for a blessing! (It is best to avoid having the child repeat a memorized prayer after you. Let her think, and make it personal.)*

d. After salvation has occurred, pray for her out loud. This is a good way to pronounce a blessing on her.

4. **Lead your child into assurance.**

Show him that he will have to keep his relationship open with God through repentance and forgiveness (just like with his family or friends), but that God will always love him ("Never will I leave you; never will I forsake you," Heb. 13:5).

* If you wish to guide your child through the prayer, here is some suggested language.

"Dear God, I know that I am a sinner [have child name specific sins he or she acknowledged earlier, such as lying, stealing, disobeying, etc.]. I know that Jesus died on the cross to pay for all my sins. I ask You to forgive me of my sins. I believe that Jesus died for me and rose from the dead, and I accept Him as my Savior. Thank You for loving me. In Jesus' name. Amen."

Cumulative Topical Index

TOPIC	SCRIPTURE	WHAT YOU'LL NEED	WHERE TO FIND IT
The Acts of the Sinful Nature and the Fruit of the Spirit	Gal. 5:19-26	3x5 cards or paper, markers, and tape	IFN, p. 43
Adding Value to Money through Saving Takes Time	Matt. 6:19-21	Supplies for making cookies and a Bible	MMK, p. 89
All Have Sinned	Rom. 3:23	Raw eggs, bucket of water	BCB, p. 89
All of Our Plans Should Match God's	Ps. 139:1-18	Paper, pencils, markers, or crayons	MMK, p. 73
As a Unique Member of God's Body, You Serve a Unique and Important Purpose	Rom. 12:4-5	Pencils, paper, a Bible	RFA, p. 103
Avoid Exasperating Children, and be Free to Raise Them in the Instruction of the Lord	Eph. 6:1-4	Rope, tape, candy, a Bible	RFA, p. 95
Avoid Things That Keep Us from Growing	Eph. 4:14-15; Heb. 5:11-14	Seeds, plants at various stages of growth or a garden or nursery to tour, Bible	CCQ, p. 77
Bad Company Corrupts Good Character	1 Cor. 15:33	Small ball, string, slips of paper, pencil, yarn or masking tape, Bible	IFN, p. 103
Be Courageous in Your Faith So You Can Be a Strong Witness for Christ	1 Cor. 16:13; James 2:14, 17	Pipe cleaners, a Bible	RFA p. 56
Be Thankful for Good Friends		Bible, art supplies, markers	IFN, p. 98
Because We Love God, We Obey His Commands		Light source, variety of objects	TC, p. 23
Being Content with What We Have	Phil. 4:11-13	Bible	CCQ, p. 17
Being Diligent Means Working Hard and Well	Gen. 39–41	Bible, paper, a pencil and other supplies depending on jobs chosen	MMK, p. 64

TOPIC	SCRIPTURE	WHAT YOU'LL NEED	WHERE TO FIND IT
Being a Faithful Steward Means Managing God's Gifts Wisely	1 Peter 4:10; Luke 19:12-26	Graham crackers, peanut butter, thin stick pretzels, small marshmallows, and M & Ms®	MMK, p. 18
Being Jealous Means Wanting Things Other People Have	Gen. 37:4-5	Different size boxes of candy or other treats, and a Bible	OTS, p. 39
Being with God in Heaven Is Worth More than Anything Else	Matt. 13:44-46	Hershey's kisses candies, a Bible	NTS, p. 24
Budgeting Means Making a Plan for Using Our Money	Jud. 6–7	Table, large sheets or paper, and markers or crayons	MMK, p. 79
Budgeting Means the Money Coming in Has to Equal the Money Going Out	Luke 14:28-35; Jud. 6–7	Supply of beans, paper, pencil, and Bible	MMK, p. 80
By Setting Aside the Time to Focus on God, We Have a Chance to Reflect on His Glory and Goodness in Our "Busy" Lives	Mark 2:27; Heb. 12:1-4	Bible, poster board, crayons and or markers, a $5 bill, tape	TC, p. 49
Change Helps Us Grow and Mature	Rom. 8:28-39	Bible	WLS, p. 39
Change Is Good	1 Kings 17:8-16	Jar or box for holding change, colored paper, tape, markers, Bible	MMK, p. 27
Choose Friends Who will Encourage Your Walk With God	1 Sam. 18:1-4; 23:16-18; James 2:14, 17; Prov. 27:17	Bible	RFA. p. 53
Christ Is Who We Serve	Col. 3:23-24	Paper, scissors, pens	IFN, p. 50
The Christmas Story Is about Jesus' Birth	Luke 2; Matt. 2	Styrofoam cones and balls of various sizes, a large box, markers or paints, tape, a Bible	NTS, p. 47
Christians Should Be Joyful Each Day	James 3:22-23; Ps. 118:24	Small plastic bottle, cork to fit bottle opening, water, vinegar, paper towel, Bible	CCQ, p. 67
Commitment and Hard Work Are Needed to Finish Strong	Gen. 6:5-22	Jigsaw puzzle, Bible	CCQ, p. 83

TOPIC	SCRIPTURE	WHAT YOU'LL NEED	WHERE TO FIND IT
The Consequence of Sin Is Death	Ps. 19:1-6	Dominoes	BCB, p. 57
Contentment Is the Secret to Happiness	Matt. 6:33	Package of candies, a Bible	MMK, p. 51
Creation	Gen. 1:1; Ps. 19:1-6; Rom. 1:20	Nature book or video, Bible	IFN, p. 17
David and Bathsheba	2 Sam. 11:1–12:14	Bible	BCB, p. 90
Description of Heaven	Rev. 21:3-4, 10-27	Bible, drawing supplies	BCB, p. 76
Difficulty Can Help Us Grow	Jer. 32:17; Luke 18:27	Bible, card game like Old Maid or Crazy Eights	CCQ, p. 33
Discipline and Training Make Us Stronger	Prov. 4:23	Narrow doorway, Bible	CCQ, p. 103
Dishonesty Teaches Others to Distrust Us	Prov. 12:13	Small pebbles, eggs, a spoon, Bible	P, p. 29
Do Not Give In to Those Around You	Matt. 14:6-12; Luke 23:13-25	Empty one two-liter plastic bottles, eye-dropper, water, a Bible	SS, p.21
Don't Be Distracted by Unimportant Things	Matt. 14:22-32	One marked penny, lots of unmarked pennies, a wrapped gift for each child, a Bible	NTS, p. 35
Don't Be Yoked with Unbelievers	2 Cor. 16:17–17:1	Milk, food coloring	IFN, p. 105
Don't Give Respect Based on Material Wealth	Eph. 6:1-8; 1 Peter 2:13-17; Ps. 119:17; James 2:1-2; 1 Tim. 4:12	Large sheet of paper, tape, a pen, Bible	IFN, p. 64
Dorcas Made Clothes and Did Good Things	Acts 9:36-42	Large pillowcases, fabric markers, scissors, a Bible	NTS, p. 71
Easter Was God's Plan for Jesus	John 3:16; Rom. 3:23; 6:23	Paper and pencils or pens, materials to make a large cross, and a Bible	HFN, p. 27
Equality Does Not Mean Contentment	Matt. 20:1-16	Money or candy bars, tape recorder or radio, Bible	WLS, p. 21
Even if We're Not in the Majority, We May Be Right	2 Tim. 3:12-17	Piece of paper, pencil, water	CCQ, p. 95
Every Day Is a Gift from God	Prov. 16:9	Bible	CCQ, p. 69
Evil Hearts Say Evil Words	Prov. 15:2-8; Luke 6:45; Eph. 4:29	Bible, small mirror	IFN, p. 79

TOPIC	SCRIPTURE	WHAT YOU'LL NEED	WHERE TO FIND IT
Expect Mood Swings, but Learn to Control Your Attitude	Matt 5:1-22	Aluminum foil, a Bible	RFA, p. 61
Family Members Ought to Be Loyal to Each Other	The Book of Ruth	Shoebox, two pieces of different colored felt, seven pipe cleaners (preferably of different colors)	OTS, p. 67
Fearing God Means Being in Awe of Him and Respecting Him	Prov. 28:14	Bowl, water, pepper, soft soap, Bible	P, p. 85
Friends Sharpen One Another by Being Loyal, Unselfish, Willing to Learn, and Forgiving	Prov. 17:9, 17; 27:6, 17	Candles, matches, construction paper, permanent black marker, tape, a Bible	P, p. 71
The Fruit of the Spirit	Gal. 5:22-23; Luke 3:8; Acts 26:20	Blindfold and Bible	BCB, p. 92
God Allows Testing to Help Us Mature	James 1:2-4	Bible	BCB, p. 44
God Became a Man So We Could Understand His Love	John 14:9-10	A pet of some kind, and a Bible	HFN, p. 85
God Can Clean Our Guilty Consciences	1 John 1:9	Small dish of bleach, dark piece of material, Bible	WLS, p. 95
God Can Do the Impossible	John 6:1-14	Bible, sturdy plank (6 or more inches wide and 6 to 8 feet long), a brick or similar object, snack of fish and crackers	CCQ, p. 31
God Can Give Us Strength		Musical instruments (or pots and pans with wooden spoons) and a snack	OTS, p. 52
God Can Guide Us Away from Satan's Traps	Ps. 119:9-11; Prov. 3:5-6	Ten or more inexpensive mousetraps, pencil, blindfold, Bible	WLS, p. 72
God Can Help Us Knock Sin Out of Our Lives	Ps. 32:1-5; 1 John 1:9	Heavy drinking glass, pie tin, small slips of paper, pencils, large raw egg, cardboard tube from a roll of toilet paper, broom, masking tape, Bible	WLS, p. 53

TOPIC	SCRIPTURE	WHAT YOU'LL NEED	WHERE TO FIND IT
God Can Use Us in Unique Ways to Accomplish His Plans		Strings of cloth, clothespins or strong tape, "glow sticks" or small flashlights	OTS, p. 63
God Cares for Us Even in Hard Times	Job 1–2; 42	Bible	WLS, p. 103
God Chose to Make Dads (or Moms) as a Picture of Himself	Gen. 1:26-27	Large sheets of paper, pencils, a bright light, a picture of your family, a Bible	HFN, p. 47
God Commands Honoring for Our Benefit	Luke 15:11-32; Ex. 20:12; Deut. 5:16	Bibles	TC, p. 56
God Created the Heavens and the Earth	Gen. 1	Small tent or sheet and a rope, Christmas lights, two buckets (one with water), a coffee can with dirt, a tape recorder and cassette, and a flashlight	OTS, p. 17
God Created Us	Isa. 45:9, 64:8; Ps. 139:13	Bible and video of potter with clay	BCB, p. 43
God Created the World, Stars, Plants, Animals, and People	Gen. 1	Play dough or clay, safe shaping or cutting tools, a Bible	OTS, p. 19
God Doesn't Like Laziness	Prov. 22:13; 6:9; 13:4; 21:25; 18:9; 12:27; 20:17; 11:18; 10:4; 14:23; 15:19; 19:15; 10:5	Microwave popcorn, microwave oven (or supplies for popping corn on the stove), Bible	P, p. 59
God Doesn't See Us the Way the World Does—He Looks at the Heart	Ex. 20:16; 1 Sam. 16:7	Copies of the "Optical Illusions" page, a Bible	RFA, p. 23
God Doesn't Want Us to Worry	Matt. 6:25-34; Phil. 4:6-7; Ps. 55:22	Bible, paper, pencils	CCQ, p. 39
God Forgives Those Who Confess Their Sins	1 John 1:9	Sheets of paper, tape, Bible	BCB, p. 58
God Gave Jesus a Message for Us	John 1:14,18; 8:19; 12:49-50	Goldfish in water or bug in jar, water	BCB, p. 66
God Gives and God Can Take Away	Luke 12:13-21	Bible, timer with bell or buzzer, large bowl of small candies, smaller bowl for each child	CCQ, p. 15
God Gives Us the Skills We Need to Do What He Asks of Us		Materials to make a sling (cloth, shoestrings), plastic golf balls or marshmallows, stuffed animals	OTS, p. 73

TOPIC	SCRIPTURE	WHAT YOU'LL NEED	WHERE TO FIND IT
God Has Given Us Sex As a Gift Only to Be Shared with Our Spouse	1 Cor. 6;18-20	Cake donuts, string, chocolate syrup, towels, a Bible	RFA, p. 37
God Is Greater Than We Can Understand; Yet He Reveals Himself to Us through His Word	Prov. 15:3, 8-9, 11, 25, 29;16:2, 33; 17:3, 5; 11:8, 21, 31;18:10; 21:27; 22-23; 28:29	Empty wine bottle, cork, cloth napkin, Bible	P, p. 83
God Is Holy	Ex. 3:1-6	Masking tape, baby powder or corn starch, broom, Bible	IFN, p. 31
God Is Invisible, Powerful, and Real	John 1:18, 4:24; Luke 24:36-39	Balloons, balls, refrigerator magnets, Bible	IFN, p. 15
God Is the Source of Our Strength	Jud. 16	Oversized sweat-shirt, balloons, mop heads or other items to use as whigs, items to stack to make pillars, a Bible	OTS, p. 61
God Is Our Only Source of Strength	Isa. 40:29-31	Straws, fresh baking potatoes, a Bible	SS, p.33
God Is with Us	Ex. 25:10-22; Deut. 10:1-5; Josh. 3:14-17; 1 Sam. 3:3; 2 Sam. 6:12-15	A large cardboard box, two broom han-dles, a utility knife, strong tape, gold spray paint, and a Bible	OTS, p. 49
God Keeps His Promises	Gen. 6–9:16	Plastic coffee can lid, flashlight, bubble solution, straw, a Bible	SS, p.75
God Keeps His Promises	Gen. 9:13, 15	Sheets of colored cel-lophane, cardboard, scissors, tape, a Bible, a lamp or large flashlight	OTS, p. 25
God Knew His Plans for Us	Jer. 29:11	Two puzzles and a Bible	BCB, p. 19
God Knew Moses Would Be Found by Pharaoh's Daughter	Ex. 2:1-10	A doll or stuffed animal, a basket, and a blanket	OTS, p. 43
God Knows All about Us	Ps. 139:2-4; Matt. 10:30	3x5 cards, a pen	BCB, p. 17
God Knows Everything	Isa. 40:13-14; Eph. 4:1-6	Bible	IFN, p. 15
God Knows the Plan for Our Lives	Rom. 8:28	Three different 25–50 piece jigsaw puzzles, Bible	WLS, p. 101

Family Night
TOOL CHEST

AN INTRODUCTION TO FAMILY NIGHTS
= IFN

BASIC CHRISTIAN BELIEFS
= BCB

CHRISTIAN CHARACTER QUALITIES
= CCQ

WISDOM LIFE SKILLS
= WLS

MONEY MATTERS FOR KIDS
= MMK

HOLIDAYS FAMILY NIGHT
= HFN

BIBLE STORIES FOR PRESCHOOLERS (OLD TESTAMENT)
= OTS

SIMPLE SCIENCE
= SS

BIBLE STORIES FOR PRESCHOOLERS (NEW TESTAMENT)
= NTS

TEN COMMANDMENTS
= TC

PROVERBS
= P

READY FOR ADOLESENCE
= RFA

TOPIC	SCRIPTURE	WHAT YOU'LL NEED	WHERE TO FIND IT
God Looks at the Heart	1 Sam. 16:7; Gal. 2:6	4 cans of pop (2 regular and 2 diet), 1 large tub, duct tape, water, a Bible	SS, p. 81
God Looks beyond the Mask and into Our Hearts		Costumes	HFN, p. 65
God Loves It When We Use the Gifts He's Given Us to Help Others	Prov. 11:24; 14:21	Box of tools, Bible	P, p. 72
God Loves and Protects Us	Matt. 6:26-27	One or two raw eggs, a sink or bucket, a Bible	SS, p. 15
God Loves Us So Much, He Sent Jesus	John 3:16; Eph. 2:8-9	I.O.U. for each family member	IFN, p. 34
God Made Our Family Unique by Placing Each of Us in It		Different color paint for each family member, toothpicks or paintbrushes to dip into paint, white paper, Bible	BCB, p. 110
God Made Us		Building blocks, such as Tinkertoys, Legos, or K'nex	HFN, p. 15
God Made Us in His Image	Gen. 1:24-27	Play dough or clay and Bible	BCB, p. 24
God Never Changes	Ecc. 3:1-8; Heb. 13:8	Paper, pencils, Bible	WLS, p. 37
God Owns Everything; He Gives Us Things to Manage		Large sheet of poster board or newsprint and colored markers	MMK, p. 17
God Points Us toward His Plan	Prov. 13:13; 24:10; 27:21; 22:17-19; 29:25	Construction paper, tape, glue, Bible	P, p. 54
God Provides a Way Out of Temptation	1 Cor. 10:12-13; James 1:13-14; 4:7; 1 John 2:15-17	Bible	IFN, p. 88
God Sees Who We Really Are—We Can Never Fool Him	1 Sam. 16:7	Construction paper, scissors, crayons or markers, a hat or bowl, and a Bible	HFN, p. 66
God Strengthens Us and Protects Us from Satan	2 Thes. 3:3; Ps. 18:2-3	Two un-inflated black balloons, water, a candle, matches, a Bible	SS, p. 16
God Teaches Us about Love through Others	1 Cor. 13	Colored paper, markers, crayons, scissors, tape or glue, and a Bible	HFN, p. 22

TOPIC	SCRIPTURE	WHAT YOU'LL NEED	WHERE TO FIND IT
God Used Plagues to Tell Pharaoh to Let Moses and His People Go	Ex. 7–12	A clear glass, red food coloring, water, and a Bible	OTS, p. 44
God Uses Many Ways to Get Our Attention	Dan. 5	Large sheets of paper or poster board, tape, finger-paint, and a Bible	OTS, p. 79
God Wants Our Best Effort in All We Do	Col. 3:23-24	Children's blocks or a large supply of cardboard boxes	MMK, p. 63
God Wants a Passionate Relationship with Us	Rev. 3:16	Pans of hot, cold, and lukewarm water, hot and cold drinks	SS, p. 69
God Wants Us to Be Diligent in Our Work	Prov. 6:6-11; 1 Thes. 4:11-12	Video about ants or picture books or encyclopedia, Bible	CCQ, p. 55
God Wants Us to Be Moldable	Prov. 29:1	Flour, alum, salad oil, salt, boiling water, a Bible	P, p. 67
God Wants Us to Get Closer to Him	James 4:8; 1 John 4:7-12	Hidden Bibles, clues to find them	BCB, p. 33
God Wants Us to Give to Others in Love		Candy	NTS, p. 54
God Wants Us to Glorify Him	Ps. 24:1; Luke 12:13-21	Paper, pencils, Bible	WLS, p. 47
God Wants Us to Reflect His Word	James 1:19-25	Bible, hand mirror, cardboard, a flashlight	NTS, p. 84
God Wants Us to Work and Be Helpful	2 Thes. 3:6-15	Several undone chores, Bible	CCQ, p. 53
God Will Never Leave Us or Forsake Us	Matt. 28:20	Long sheet of paper, pencil, scissors, tape or glue, a Bible	SS, p. 76
God Will Send the Holy Spirit	John 14:23-26; 1 Cor. 2:12	Flashlights, small treats, Bible	IFN, p. 39
God Will Separate Those Who Believe in Jesus from Those Who Don't	Matt. 13:47-49; John 3:16	Large box, crayons or markers, a large bath towel, candy-size rocks, candy, wax paper, a Bible	NTS, p. 29
God Will Separate Those Who Love Him from Those Who Don't	Matt. 25:31-46	Coarse salt, ground pepper, plastic spoon, wool cloth, a Bible	SS, p. 64
God's Covenant with Noah	Gen. 8:13-21; 9:8-17	Bible, paper, crayons or markers	BCB, p. 52
God's Name Represents His Character, Person-age, Nature, Reputa-tion, and Role	Ex. 20:7; Matt. 5:34	Dictionary, paper, pencils, a Bible	TC, p. 41

TOPIC	SCRIPTURE	WHAT YOU'LL NEED	WHERE TO FIND IT
God's View of Righteous Living Is Not the Same as the World's View of Successful Living	Matt. 5:3-12	Table settings, a Bible	RFA, p. 77
A Good Friend Encourages Us to Do What Jesus Would Do	Ecc. 4:9-12	Strips of cardboard, books, 50 pennies, a Bible	SS, p. 82
Greater Freedom Requires Greater Responsibility	Luke 16:10	Shoebox, flat plate, golf ball, a Bible	RFA, p. 65
Grow and Develop as Jesus Did—Physical, Mental, Spiritual, and Social	Luke 2:52	Soda straws (50 or more per child), a Bible	RFA, p. 15
Guarding the Gate to Our Minds	Prov. 4:13; 2 Cor. 11:3; Phil. 4:8	Bible, poster board for each family member, old magazines, glue, scissors, markers	CCQ, p. 23
The Holy Spirit Helps Us	Eph. 1:17; John 14:15-17; Acts 1:1-11; Eph. 3:16-17; Rom. 8:26-27; 1 Cor. 2:11-16	Bible	BCB, p. 99
The Holy Spirit Helps Us to Be a Light in the Dark World	Matt. 5:14-16; 1 Tim. 2:1-4	Wintergreen or Cryst-O-Mint Lifesavers, a Bible	SS, p. 40
Honesty Means Being Sure We Tell the Truth and Are Fair	Prov. 10:9; 11:3; 12:5; 14:2; 28:13	A bunch of coins and a Bible	MMK, p. 58
Honor the Holy Spirit, Don't Block Him	1 John 4:4; 1 Cor. 6:19-20	Bible, blow-dryer or vacuum cleaner with exit hose, a Ping-Pong ball	CCQ, p. 47
Honor Your Parents	Ex. 20:12	Paper, pencil, treats, umbrella, soft objects, masking tape, pen, Bible	IFN, p. 55
Honoring Your Parents Teaches You to Honor God		Balloon, two different pieces of colored paper, pencils	TC, p. 55
How Big Is an Ark?		Large open area, buckets of water, cans of animal food, bags of dog food, and four flags	OTS, p. 24
A Humble Heart Pleases God	Prov. 15:33; 16:5, 18; 29:23	Handout of cutout, a Bible	P, p. 33

TOPIC	SCRIPTURE	WHAT YOU'LL NEED	WHERE TO FIND IT
Idols Come in All Shapes and Sizes	Isa. 46:1-11; Col. 3:5-6	A favorite thing from each child	TC, p. 37
If We Accept Jesus as Savior, We'll Get into Heaven	Rev. 20:15, 21:27	Bible, marshmallows, cotton candy, ice cream	NTS, p. 90
If We Confess Our Sins, Jesus Will Forgive Us	Heb. 12:1;1 John 1:9	Magic slate, candies, paper, pencils, bathrobe ties or soft rope, items to weigh someone down, and a Bible	HFN, p. 28
The Importance of Your Name Being Written in the Book of Life	Rev. 20:11-15; 21:27	Bible, phone book, access to other books with family name	BCB, p. 74
Intent to Commit Sexual Sin Is as Wrong as the Act Itself	Matt. 5:27-28; Ps. 119:9	Three large boxes and a Bible	TC, p. 69
Investing and Saving Adds Value to Money	Prov. 21:20	Two and a half dollars for each family member	MMK, p. 87
It Is Important to Spend Time Praising God	Ps. 66:1; 81:1; 95:1; 98:4; 100:1	Plastic straws, scissors, a Bible	SS, p. 52
It's Better to Follow the Truth	Rom. 1:25; Prov. 2:1-5	Second set of clues, box of candy or treats, Bible	WLS, p. 86
It's Better to Wait for Something Than to Borrow Money to Buy It	2 Kings 4:1-7; Prov. 22:7	Magazines, advertisements, paper, a pencil, Bible	MMK, p. 103
It's Difficult to Be a Giver When You're a Debtor		Pennies or other coins	MMK, p. 105
It's Easy to Follow a Lie, but It Leads to Disappointment		Clues as described in lesson, empty box	WLS, p. 85
It Is a Good Thing to Say Encouraging Words	Prov. 16:24; 27:6; 13:14; 18:21	Colorfully decorated boxes, stickers, paper, pens or pencils, Bible	P, p. 48
It's Important to Listen to Jesus' Message		Bible	BCB, p. 68
It's Not Always Easy to Do What Jesus Wants Us to Do	Matt. 7:13	Toy blocks, a narrow board, two cinder blocks, a Bible	NTS, p. 17
It's Not Easy to Break a Pattern of Sin	James 1:12-15	Paper, pan, water, a Bible	SS, p. 63
It Takes Self-discipline to Fight Temptation	Prov. 6:20-24; 7:1-5	Crayons or markers, paper, Bibles	P, p. 23

Family Night
TOOL CHEST

AN INTRODUCTION TO FAMILY NIGHTS
= IFN

BASIC CHRISTIAN BELIEFS
= BCB

CHRISTIAN CHARACTER QUALITIES
= CCQ

WISDOM LIFE SKILLS
= WLS

MONEY MATTERS FOR KIDS
= MMK

HOLIDAYS FAMILY NIGHT
= HFN

BIBLE STORIES FOR PRESCHOOLERS (OLD TESTAMENT)
= OTS

SIMPLE SCIENCE
= SS

BIBLE STORIES FOR PRESCHOOLERS (NEW TESTAMENT)
= NTS

TEN COMMANDMENTS
= TC

PROVERBS
= P

READY FOR ADOLESENCE
= RFA

TOPIC	SCRIPTURE	WHAT YOU'LL NEED	WHERE TO FIND IT
It Takes Work to Have a Teachable Heart	Prov. 25:12; 12:15, 15:31; 13:18	"Medal" for each family member, Bible	P, p. 65
Jesus Came to Die for Our Sins	Rom. 5:8	A large piece of cardboard, markers, scissors, tape, and a Bible	HFN, p. 91
Jesus Came to Give Us Eternal Life	Mark 16:12-14	A calculator, a calendar, a sheet of paper, and a pencil	HFN, p. 91
Jesus Came to Teach Us about God	John 1:14, 18	Winter clothing, bread crumbs, a Bible	HFN, p. 92
Jesus Came to Show Us How Much God Loves Us	John 3:16	Supplies to make an Advent wreath, and a Bible	HFN, p. 89
Jesus Comes to Find Us When We Are Lost	Luke 15:1-7	Bible, blindfolds	NTS, p. 61
Jesus Cried Just Like We Do	John 11	Children's Bible storybook, a Bible, or video, *The Easter Promise*	NTS, p. 65
Jesus Died for Our Sins	Luke 22:1-6; Mark 14:12-26; Luke 22:47-54; Luke 22:55-62; Matt. 27:1-10; Matt. 27:11-31; Luke 23:26-34	Seven plastic eggs, slips of paper with Scripture verses, and a Bible	HFN, p. 33
Jesus Dies on the Cross	John 14:6	6-foot 2x4, 3-foot 2x4, hammers, nails, Bible	IFN, p. 33
Jesus Has Power over Death		Toilet paper rolls	NTS, p. 66
Jesus Promises Us New Bodies and a New Home in Heaven	Phil. 3:20-21; Luke 24:36-43; Rev. 21:1-4	Ingredients for making pumpkin pie, and a Bible	HFN, p. 61
Jesus Took Our Sins to the Cross and Freed Us from Being Bound Up in Sin	Rom. 6:23; 5:8; 6:18	Soft rope or heavy yarn, a watch with a second hand, thread, and a Bible	HFN, p. 53
Jesus Took the Punishment We Deserve	Rom. 6:23; John 3:16; Rom. 5:8-9	Bathrobe, list of bad deeds	IFN, p. 26
Jesus Wants Us to Do the Right Thing			NTS, p. 18
Jesus Was Victorious Over Death and Sin	Luke 23:35-43; Luke 23:44-53; Matt. 27:59-61; Luke 23:54–24:12	Five plastic eggs—four with Scripture verses, and a Bible	HFN, p. 36

TOPIC	SCRIPTURE	WHAT YOU'LL NEED	WHERE TO FIND IT
Jesus Washes His Followers' Feet	John 13:1-17	Bucket of warm soapy water, towels, Bible	IFN, p. 63
Joshua and the Battle of Jericho	Josh. 1:16-18; 6:1-21	Paper, pencil, dots on paper that, when connected, form a star	IFN, p. 57
Know Ahead of Time How You Might Respond and You Can Avoid Making Wrong Decisions under Pressure	Heb. 5:14	Three different colors of paper, three buckets, a Bible	RFA, p. 87
Knowing God's Word Helps Us Know What Stand to Take	2 Tim. 3:1-5	Current newspaper, Bible	CCQ, p. 93
Look to God, Not Others	Phil. 4:11-13	Magazines or news-papers, a chair, several pads of small yellow stickies, Bible	WLS, p. 24
Love Is Bigger than First Impressions— It Involves Commitment, Forgiveness, Understanding, and Sacrifice	2 Sam. 13:1-2, 14-15; 1 Cor. 13:4-8	Several types of soft drinks, coffee, tea, paper cups, a Bible	RFA, p. 45
Love Is Unselfish	1 Cor. 13	A snack and a Bible	HFN, p. 21
Love Means Putting Others' Needs above Our Own	Luke 10:25-37	Children's Bible storybook, two equal-length strips of wood, paper, marker, costumes, a Bible	NTS, p. 53
Loving Money Is Wrong	1 Tim. 6:6-10	Several rolls of coins, masking tape, Bible	WLS, p. 45
Lying Can Hurt People	Acts 5:1-11	Two pizza boxes— one empty and one with a fresh pizza— and a Bible	MMK, p. 57
Lying Has Consequences	Ex. 20:16; Matt. 5:37	Baseball bat or stick of same length, masking tape, Bible	TC, p. 81
Meeting Goals Requires Planning	Prov. 3:5-6	Paper, scissors, pen-cils, a treat, a Bible	MMK, p. 71
Mentors Can Help Us Navigate through Life's Situations	Heb. 13:7; 2 Peter 3:18; Ecc. 4:9-12; 1 Tim. 3:1-7	Balsa wood air-planes, small Post-It-Notes, a Bible	RFA, p. 71

TOPIC	SCRIPTURE	WHAT YOU'LL NEED	WHERE TO FIND IT
Mood Swings Are a Part of Adolescence, but When We Focus on God, Everything Gains Proper Perspective	Prov. 3:5-6	Balloons, a Bible	RFA, p. 47
Moms Are Special and Important to Us and to God	Prov. 24:3-4	Confetti, streamers, a comfortable chair, a wash basin with warm water, two cloths, and a Bible	HFN, p. 41
Moms Model Jesus' Love When They Serve Gladly	2 Tim. 1:4-7	Various objects depending on chosen activity and a Bible	HFN, p. 42
Money and Worldly Accomplishments Don't Make Us Successful in God's Eyes	Prov. 12:3; 25:27; 27:2	Sturdy board or table leaf, blindfold, Bible	P, p. 77
The More We Know God, the More We Know His Voice	John 10:1-6	Bible	BCB, p. 35
Murders, and the Attitude that Causes People to Murder, Is Sinful	Ex. 20:13; Matt. 22:37-39; Gen. 4:8-10	Pennies and a Bible	TC, p. 61
Nicodemus Asks Jesus about Being Born Again	John 3:7, 50-51; 19:39-40	Bible, paper, pencil, costume	BCB, p. 81
Noah Obeyed God When He Built the Ark	Gen. 6:14-16	A large refrigerator box, markers or paints, self-adhesive paper, stuffed animals, a Bible, utility knife	OTS, p. 23
Nothing Is Impossible When It Is in God's Will	Matt. 21:28	Hard-boiled egg, butter, glass bottle, paper, matches, a Bible	SS, p. 34
Obedience Has Good Rewards		Planned outing everyone will enjoy, directions on 3x5 cards, number cards	IFN, p. 59
Obey God First		Paper, markers, scissors, and blindfolds	OTS, p. 80
Only a Relationship with God Can Fill Our Need	Isa. 55:1-2	Doll that requires batteries, batteries for the doll, dollar bill, pictures of a house, an expensive car, and a pretty woman or handsome man, Bible	WLS, p. 62

TOPIC	SCRIPTURE	WHAT YOU'LL NEED	WHERE TO FIND IT
Only God Can Provide for Our Needs	Ex. 20:4-6	Items representing children's favorite media stars and a Bible	TC, p. 35
Open Communication Is Vital to Healthy Relationships between Children and ParentsOur Identity Is Found in Christ, Not the World	Prov. 4:1-9; 6:20-23; Ps. 103:13; Deut. 6:47	Paper, a Bible	RFA, p. 93
Our Actions Should Mirror God, Not the World	Rom. 12:2	Regular glass, dried peas, a wine glass, a pie tin, water, a Bible	SS, p. 57
Our Conscience Helps Us Know Right from Wrong	Rom. 2:14-15	Foods with a strong smell, blindfold, Bible	WLS, p. 93
Our Identity Is Found in Christ, Not the World	2 Cor. 5:17-20; 6:3-10	Pencils, Paper, a Bible	RFA, p. 101
Our Minds Should Be Filled with Good, Not Evil	Phil 4:8; Ps. 119:9, 11	Bible, bucket of water, several large rocks	CCQ, p. 26
Our Tongue Is Powerful and Should Be Used to Glorify God	James 3:5-8	Squirt gun, pie pan, Pop Rocks candy, a Bible	SS, p. 51
Parable of the Talents	Matt. 25:14-30	Bible	IFN, p. 73
Parable of the Vine and Branches	John 15:1-8	Tree branch, paper, pencils, Bible	IFN, p. 95
People Came to See Jesus and Bring Him Gifts	Luke 2; Matt. 2	Styrofoam cones and balls of various sizes, a large box, markers or paints, tape, a Bible	NTS, p. 48
People, Like Plants, Need Good Soil to Grow	Mark 4:3-8, 13-20	Cake pan, aluminum foil, small stones, seeds, toothpicks, potting soil, a Bible	NTS, p. 41
People Look at Outside Appearance, but God Looks at the Heart	1 Sam. 17	Slings from activity on p. 73, plastic golf balls or marshmallows, a tape measure, cardboard, markers, and a Bible	OTS, p. 75
People Who Have the Gift of Hospitality Open Their Homes and Serve Others		Snacks and supplies for a nice meal	NTS, p. 78

TOPIC	SCRIPTURE	WHAT YOU'LL NEED	WHERE TO FIND IT
Persecution Brings a Reward		Bucket, bag of ice, marker, one-dollar bill	WLS, p. 32
Planning Helps Us Finish Strong	Phil. 3:10-14	Flight map on p. 86, paper, pencils, Bible	CCQ, p. 85
Pray, Endure, and Be Glad When We're Persecuted	Matt. 5:11-12, 44; Rom. 12:14; 1 Cor. 4:12	Notes, Bible, candle or flashlight, dark small space	WLS, p. 29
Prayer Keeps Us Connected to God	Prov. 15:29	Wooden 6- to 12-inch dowel 1/4" in diameter, paper, tape, Bible	P, p. 53
Priscilla Had the Gift of Hospitality	Acts 18:1-4; 18-26; Rom. 16:3-5	Large sheet, rope, clothespins, a Bible	NTS, p. 77
Problems Are Inevitable, but with God's Help, We Can Learn from Difficult Experiences	James 1: 2-4	Snap-together model or simple puzzle, a Bible	RFA, p. 31
Proverbs Teaches Us How to Live Godly Lives	Prov. 1:1-7	Ingredients for baking a cake, Bible	P, p.15
Putting God First Builds a Solid Relationship	Mark 6:35; Luke 4:16; Mark 13:31; Luke 12:31	Wide-mouth glass jar, large rocks, sand, water, permanent marker, a Bible	SS, p. 70
Remember All God Has Done for You	Ex. 25:1; 16:34; Num. 17:10; Deut. 31:26	Ark of the covenant from p. 49, cardboard or Styrofoam, crackers, a stick, and a Bible	OTS, p. 51
Remember What God Has Done for You	Gen. 12:7-8; 13:18; 22:9	Bricks or large rocks, paint, and a Bible	OTS, p. 31
The Responsibilities of Families	Eph. 5:22-33; 6:1-4	Photo albums, Bible	BCB, p. 101
The Road of the Foolish Is Hard; the Road of the Wise Has Rewards	Prov. 10:21; 14:15-16; 15:14; 16:16, 22; 17:10; 19:25; 29:8, 11	Paper cups, a 4-foot-long 2x4, a food prize, Bible	P, p. 41
Satan Looks for Ways to Trap Us	Luke 4:1-13	Cardboard box, string, stick, small ball, Bible	WLS, p. 69
Seek God's Will and Learn Not to Follow your Emotions	John 14:17, 26; 1 Cor. 2:9-12; Matt. 6:33	Balloons, broom, fan, a Bible	RFA, p. 63
Self-control Helps Us Resist the Enemy	1 Peter 5:8-9; 1 Peter 2:11-12	Blindfold, watch or timer, feather or other "tickly" item, Bible	CCQ, p. 101
Serve One Another in Love	Gal. 5:13	Bag of small candies, at least three per child	IFN, p. 47

TOPIC	SCRIPTURE	WHAT YOU'LL NEED	WHERE TO FIND IT
Sex Was Given to Adults as a Gift to Be Enjoyed Only in Marriage, as a True Sign of Commitment and Trust	1 Thes. 4:3-8; Ex. 20:4-6	Child's favorite wrapped candy, masking tape, a Bible	TC, p. 67
Share God's Love with Others So They Can Join Us in Heaven		Rocks, plastic bags, paper, pencils	NTS, p. 30
Sin and Busyness Interfere with Our Prayers	Luke 10:38-42; Ps. 46:10; Matt. 5:23-24; 1 Peter 3:7	Bible, two paper cups, two paper clips, long length of fishing line	CCQ, p. 61
Sin Separates Humanity	Gen. 3:1-24	Bible, clay creations, piece of hardened clay or play dough	BCB, p. 25
Some Places Aren't Open to Everyone		Book or magazine with "knock-knock" jokes	BCB, p. 73
Some Things in Life Are Out of Our Control		Blindfolds	BCB, p. 41
Sometimes God Surprises Us with Great Things	Gen. 15:15	Large sheet of poster board, straight pins or straightened paper clips, a flashlight, and a Bible	OTS, p. 32
Sometimes We Face Things That Seem Impossible		Bunch of cardboard boxes or blocks	OTS, p. 55
Sour Words Can Hurt Other People	Prov. 6:16-19; 15:4	Lemon slices, glasses of water, Bible	P, p. 47
Stand Strong in the Lord	Prov. 1:8-10; 12:3	A jar, string, chair, fan, small weight, a Bible	SS, p. 22
Temptation Takes Our Eyes Off God		Fishing pole, items to catch, timer, Bible	IFN, p. 85
The Ten Commandments Are the Standards for How God Wants Us to Live		Target with 10 holes, balls, bean bags or rolled socks	TC, p. 15
The Ten Commandments Help Us to Identify What Sin Is in Today's World	Ex. 20	Paper, pens or pencils, and a Bible	TC, p. 21
The Ten Commandments Show Us Our Sinfulness and Our Need for a Savior	Rom. 3:20; 7:7-20	Butcher paper, pens, measuring tape, and a Bible	TC, p. 17
Test What the World Offers for Consistency with Jesus' Teachings	1 John 4:1	Candle, apple, almond, a Bible	SS, p. 58

Family Night
TOOL CHEST

AN INTRODUCTION TO FAMILY NIGHTS
= IFN

BASIC CHRISTIAN BELIEFS
= BCB

CHRISTIAN CHARACTER QUALITIES
= CCQ

WISDOM LIFE SKILLS
= WLS

MONEY MATTERS FOR KIDS
= MMK

HOLIDAYS FAMILY NIGHT
= HFN

BIBLE STORIES FOR PRESCHOOLERS (OLD TESTAMENT)
= OTS

SIMPLE SCIENCE
= SS

BIBLE STORIES FOR PRESCHOOLERS (NEW TESTAMENT)
= NTS

TEN COMMANDMENTS
= TC

PROVERBS
= P

READY FOR ADOLESCENCE
= RFA

TOPIC	SCRIPTURE	WHAT YOU'LL NEED	WHERE TO FIND IT
There Are Only Two Things That Will Last, People (Relationships) and God's Word	Matt. 6:33	Paper, markers, a Bible	TC, p. 87
There Is a Difference between Needs and Wants	Prov. 31:16; Matt. 6:21	Paper, pencils, glasses of drinking water, a soft drink	MMK, p. 95
There Is Only One True God We Can Trust and Believe In	Ex. 20:3	Small cups that look identical, a small object (such as a ball), a Bible	TC, p. 27
Things That Are Important to Us Don't Always Cost a Lot of Money		Stuffed toy, candy bar, toys, etc.	NTS, p. 23
Those Who Don't Believe Are Foolish	Ps. 44:1	Ten small pieces of paper, pencil, Bible	IFN, p. 19
A Time of Rest Helps Us to Refocus on God and Brings Purpose to All Our Weekly Activity— to Serve Him	Gen. 2:2-3; Ex. 20:8-11; 31:12-17	Bible, balloons, markers, 1 small stone per child, paper, and pencils	TC, p. 47
Tithing Means Giving One-Tenth Back to God	Gen. 28:10-22; Ps. 3:9-10	All family members need ten similar items each, a Bible	MMK, p. 33
To Get to Heaven, Your Name Must Be in the Book of Life		Phone book, paper, crayons or markers	NTS, p. 89
The Tongue Is Small but Powerful	James 3:3-12	Video, news magazine or picture book showing devastation of fire, match, candle, Bible	IFN, p. 77
The Treasure of a Thankful Heart Is Contentment	Eph. 5:20	3x5 cards, pencils, fun prizes, and a Bible	HFN, p. 72
Trials Help Us Grow	James 1:2-4	Sugar cookie dough, cookie cutters, baking sheets, miscellaneous baking supplies, Bible	WLS, p. 15
Trials Test How We've Grown	James 1:12	Bible	WLS, p. 17
Trust Is Important	Matt. 6:25-34	Each person needs an item he or she greatly values	MMK, p. 25
The Truth Is a Delight to God	Prov. 6:16-19; 11:1; Ex.20:16; Prov.12:19	Small candies, rubber bands, large serving spoons, a cloth napkin, a marker, Bible	P, p. 27

TOPIC	SCRIPTURE	WHAT YOU'LL NEED	WHERE TO FIND IT
We Can Love by Helping Those in Need	Heb. 13:1-3		IFN, p. 48
We Can Show Love through Respecting Family Members		Paper and pen	IFN, p. 66
We Can't Hide from God		Supplies will vary	OTS, p. 85
We Can't Take Back the Damage of Our Words		Tube of toothpaste for each child, $10 bill	IFN, p. 78
We Deserve Punishment for Our Sins	Rom. 6:23	Dessert, other materials as decided	IFN, p. 24
We Give to God because We're Thankful		Supplies for a celebration dinner, also money for each family member	MMK, p. 36
We Have All We Need in Our Lives	Ecc. 3:11	Paper, pencils, Bible	WLS, p. 61
We Have a New Life in Christ	John 3:3; 2 Cor. 5:17	Video or picture book of caterpillar forming a cocoon then a butterfly, or a tadpole becoming a frog, or a seed becoming a plant	BCB, p. 93
We Have Much to Be Thankful For	1 Chron. 16:4-36	Unpopped popcorn, a bowl, supplies for popping popcorn, and a Bible	HFN, p. 79
We Know Others by Our Relationships with Them		Copies of questionnaire, pencils, Bible	BCB, p. 31
We Must Be in Constant Contact with God		Blindfold	CCQ, p. 63
We Must Choose to Obey		3x5 cards or slips of paper, markers, and tape	IFN, p. 43
We Must Either Choose Christ or Reject Christ	Matt. 12:30	Clear glass jar, cooking oil, water, spoon, Bible	CCQ, p. 96
We Must Give Thanks in All Circumstances	1 Thes. 5:18	A typical family meal, cloth strips, and a Bible	HFN, p. 77
We Must Guard Our Minds against Temptation	Prov. 5:1-2, 7-8, 21-23	Golf balls, blanket, empty coffee cans, Bible	P, p. 21
We Must Hold Firm to Our Faith and Depend on God for Strength	Eph. 6:16	Balloons, long darts or shish kebab skewers, cooking oil, a Bible	SS, p. 27

TOPIC	SCRIPTURE	WHAT YOU'LL NEED	WHERE TO FIND IT
We Must Learn How Much Responsibility We Can Handle		Building blocks, watch with second hand, paper, pencil	IFN, p. 71
We Must Listen	Prov. 1:5; 8-9; 4:1	Bible, other supplies for the task you choose	WLS, p. 77
We Must "Root" Ourselves in Jesus and Live by God's Word	Mark 4:1-24	A potted plant, light-weight cardboard, crayons, scissors, a Bible	NTS, p. 42
We Must Stay Focused on Jesus So We Don't Fall		Masking tape	NTS, p. 36
We Must Think Before We Speak	James 1:19	Bible	WLS, p. 79
We Must Work Hard to Become Wise One Step at a Time	Prov. 1:3-7; 19:25; 12:11; 29:11; 10:13; 15:21	Big box, lots of heavy books, Bible	P, p. 43
We Must Work Hard to Learn from the Proverbs and Gain Wisdom	Prov. 1:7	Toothpicks, Bible	P, p. 16
We Need to Feed on God's Word to Grow in Christ	Ps. 119:105; 2 Chron. 34:31; Acts 17:11; James 1:22-25	Raisins, clear drinking glass, a two-liter bottle of clear soft drink, a Bible	SS, p. 46
We Need to Grow Closer to Jesus Each Day	Acts 9:1-18	Pitcher, lemonade mix (sugarless), sugar, dry ice, a Bible	SS, p. 45
We Need to Grow Physically, Emotionally, and Spiritually	1 Peter 2:2	Photograph albums or videos of your children at different ages, tape measure, bathroom scale, Bible	CCQ, p. 75
We Need to Respect Each Other's Property	Ex. 20:15	Valuable family items	TC, p. 75
We Need to Treat His Name With Respect for It Represents God Who Is Holy	Ps. 99:3	Eggs, checkbook, a Bible	TC, p. 43
We Need to Try to Solve Our Differences and Forgive Before Our Attitude or Actions Become Wrongful	Matt. 5:23-26; 6:9-13	Basketballs, a bowl of M&Ms®, and a Bible	TC, p. 63
We Prove Who We Are When What We Do Reflects What We Say	James 1:22; 2:14-27	A bag of candy, a rope, and a Bible	HFN, p. 67

TOPIC	SCRIPTURE	WHAT YOU'LL NEED	WHERE TO FIND IT
We Reap What We Sow	Gal. 6:7	Candy bar, Bible	IFN, p. 55
We Should Be on Guard Against "Wanting" for True Happiness Is Not Found in Things		Pennies or candy and a box	TC, p. 88
We Should Do What God Wants Even If We Don't Think We Can		A powerful fan, large sheet of light-weight black plastic, duct tape, and a flashlight	OTS, p. 86
We Should Live God-Centered Lives	Matt. 4:10	24 dominoes or small blocks for each family member, a Bible	TC, p. 29
We Should Stamp Out Pride in Our Lives	Prov. 11:2; 13:10; 16:19; 18:12	3x5 cards, markers, Bible	P, p. 36
We Shouldn't Value Possessions Over Everything Else	1 Tim. 6:7-8	Box is optional	CCQ, p. 18
When a Sheep Is Lost, the Shepherd Finds It		Shoe box, felt, pom pom balls	NTS, p. 58
When God Sent Jesus to Earth, God Chose Me	Luke 1:26-38; John 3:16; Matt. 14:23	Going to choose a Christmas tree or other special decoration, a Bible, and hot chocolate	HFN, p. 83
When We Accept Jesus' Gift of Salvation, We Receive the Holy Spirit	John 3:5-8	1/4-full roll of toilet paper, a blow dryer, a dowel rod, a Bible	SS, p. 39
When We Apply God's Word to Our Lives, We Can Live According to God's Values	Prov. 1:3-4	2x4, a brick or other piece of wood, a Bible	RFA, p. 79
When We Focus on What We Don't Have, We Get Unhappy	1 Tim. 6:9-10; 1 Thes. 5:18; Phil. 4:11-13	A glass, water, paper, crayons, and a Bible	HFN, p. 71
When We See Something Wrong with the Way We Act We Should Fix It	James 1:22-24	Clothing, a large mirror, a Bible	NTS, p. 83
When We Surround Ourselves with Godly Friends, We Can Stand Up to Peer Pressure	Prov. 1:13-20; 18:24; 2 Cor. 6:14-18	Pennies, nickels, a dime, masking tape, table, a Bible	RFA, p. 85

TOPIC	SCRIPTURE	WHAT YOU'LL NEED	WHERE TO FIND IT
When We're Set Free from Sin, We Have the Freedom to Choose, and the Responsibility to Serve	Gal. 5:13-15	Candies, soft rope, and a Bible	HFN, p. 55
Wise Spending Means Getting Good Value for What We Buy	Luke 15:11-32	Money and a Bible	MMK, p. 97
With Help, Life Is a Lot Easier		Supplies to do the chore you choose	BCB, p. 101
With the Help of the Holy Spirit, We Can Choose to Remain Sexually Pure	1 Thes. 4:3-8	Pen, string, paper clip, a bottle	RFA, p. 39
Wolves in Sheep's' Clothing	Matt. 7:15-20	Ten paper sacks, a marker, ten small items, Bible	IFN, p. 97
Work as Unto the Lord	Prov. 28:19; 22:29; 12:14; 13:4; 6:6-8; Col. 3:23	Pinata (or supplies to make one), broomstick, Bible	P, p. 60
Worrying Doesn't Change Anything		Board, inexpensive doorbell buzzer, a 9-volt battery, extra length of electrical wire, a large belt, assorted tools	CCQ, p. 37
You Are a Product of God's Hand, Made in His Image, and You Are Uniquely Gifted	Ex. 4:10-14; Ps. 139:13-16; 1 Cor. 12:7-11; Jer. 29:11	Balloons, a Bible	RFA, p. 26
You Are Not the Only One with Adolescent Struggles	Heb. 13:5	Strips of elastic, chairs, shoes, a Bible	RFA, p. 31
You Can Choose to Obey or Not Obey, but You Can't Choose the Consequences	Josh. 6:12-17; 7:1-26	Bandanna and Bible	TC, p. 76
You Can't Go Back	Prov. 1:8-9	Four bricks, blind-folds, a couple of 2x4s, a Bible	RFA, p. 17
You Look Like the Person in Whose Image You Are Created		Paper roll, crayons, markers, pictures of your kids and of yourself as a child	BCB, p. 23

Family Night
TOOL CHEST

AN INTRODUCTION TO FAMILY NIGHTS
= IFN

BASIC CHRISTIAN BELIEFS
= BCB

CHRISTIAN CHARACTER QUALITIES
= CCQ

WISDOM LIFE SKILLS
= WLS

MONEY MATTERS FOR KIDS
= MMK

HOLIDAYS FAMILY NIGHT
= HFN

BIBLE STORIES FOR PRESCHOOLERS (OLD TESTAMENT)
= OTS

SIMPLE SCIENCE
= SS

BIBLE STORIES FOR PRESCHOOLERS (NEW TESTAMENT)
= NTS

TEN COMMANDMENTS
= TC

PROVERBS
= P

READY FOR ADOLESENCE
= RFA

Welcome to the Family!

Heritage Builders

Helping You Build a Family of Faith

We hope you've enjoyed this book. Heritage Builders was founded in 1995 by three fathers with a passion for the next generation. As a new ministry of Focus on the Family, Heritage Builders strives to equip, train and motivate parents to become intentional about building a strong spiritual heritage.

It's quite a challenge for busy parents to find ways to build a spiritual foundation for their families—especially in a way they enjoy and understand. Through activities and participation, children can learn biblical truth in a way they can understand, enjoy—and *remember*.

Passing along a heritage of Christian faith to your family is a parent's highest calling. Heritage Builders' goal is to encourage and empower you in this great mission with practical resources and inspiring ideas that really work—and help your children develop a lasting love for God.

✳✳✳

How To Reach Us

For more information, visit our Heritage Builders Web site! Log on to **www.heritagebuilders.com** to discover new resources, sample activities, and ideas to help you pass on a spiritual heritage. To request any of these resources, simply call Focus on the Family at 1-800-A-FAMILY (1-800-232-6459) or in Canada, call 1-800-661-9800. Or send your request to Focus on the Family, Colorado Springs, CO 80995. In Canada, write Focus on the Family, P.O. Box 9800, Stn. Terminal, Vancouver, B.C. V6B 4G3

To learn more about Focus on the Family or to find out if there is an associate office in your country, please visit www. family.org

We'd love to hear from you!

Try These Heritage Builders Resources!

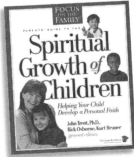

Parents' Guide to the Spiritual Growth of Children

Building a foundation of faith in your children can be easy–and fun!–with help from the ***Parents' Guide to the Spiritual Growth of Children***. Through simple and practical advice, this comprehensive guide shows you how to build a spiritual training plan for your family and it explains what to teach your children at different ages.

Bedtime Blessings

Strengthen the precious bond between you, your child and God by making ***Bedtime Blessings*** a special part of your evenings together. From best-sellingauthor John Trent, Ph.D., and Heritage Builders, this book is filled with stories, activities and blessing prayers to help you practice the biblical model of "blessing."

My Time With God

Send your child on an amazing adventure—a self-guided tour through God's Word! *My Time With God* shows your 8- to 12-year-old how to get to know God regularly in exciting ways. Through 150 days' worth of fun facts and mind-boggling trivia, prayer starters, and interesting questions, your child will discover how awesome God really is!

The Singing Bible

Children ages 2 to 7 will love *The Singing Bible,* which sets the Bible to music with over 50 fun, sing-along songs! Lead your child through Scripture by using *The Singing Bible* to introduce the story of Jonah, the Ten Commandments and more. This is a fun, fast-paced journey kids will remember!

***

Visit our Heritage Builders Web site! Log on to **www.heritagebuilders.com** to discover new resources, sample activities, and ideas to help you pass on a spiritual heritage. To request any of these resources, simply call Focus on the Family at 1-800-A-FAMILY (1-800-232-6459) or in Canada, call 1-800-661-9800. Or send your request to Focus on the Family, Colorado Springs, CO 80995. In Canada, write Focus on the Family, P.O. Box 9800, Stn. Terminal, Vancouver, B.C. V6B 4G3.

***

Every family has a heritage—a spiritual, emotional, and social legacy passed from one generation to the next. There are four main areas we at Heritage Builders recommend parents consider as they plan to pass their faith to their children:

Family Fragrance

Every family's home has a fragrance. Heritage Builders encourages parents to create a home environment that fosters a sweet, Christ-centered AROMA of love through Affection, Respect, Order, Merriment, and Affirmation.

Family Traditions

Whether you pass down stories, beliefs and/or customs, traditions can help you establish a special identity for your family. Heritage Builders encourages parents to set special "milestones" for their children to help guide them and move them through their spiritual development.

Family Compass

Parents have the unique task of setting standards for normal, healthy living through their attitudes, actions and beliefs. Heritage Builders encourages parents to give their children the moral navigation tools they need to succeed on the roads of life.

Family Moments

Creating special, teachable moments with their children is one of a parent's most precious and sometimes, most difficult responsibilities. Heritage Builders encourages parents to capture little moments throughout the day to teach and impress values, beliefs, and biblical principles onto their children.

***

We look forward to standing alongside you as you seek to impart the Lord's care and wisdom onto the next generation—onto your children.

Heritage Builders™
Helping You Build a Family of Faith

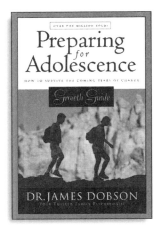
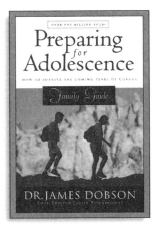
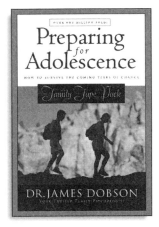
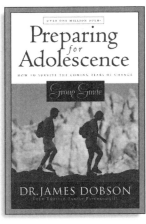
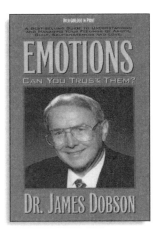
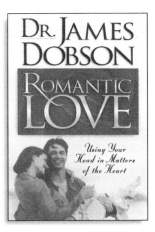